MW00883686

DON'T TALK TO THE MEDIA

29 Secrets You Need to Know Before
You Open Your Mouth to a Reporter

Gerard Braud

Cover Desgin and Interior Layout by Elizabeth Braud
www.ElizabethBraud.com
Cover Image Desgin by Cecil Cross
Cover and Interior Photos by Gerard Braud

First published by Diversified Media, LLC
January 6, 2010
Printed in the United States of America

This book is printed on acid-free paper.
ISBN: 978-1-45154-032-1

DEDICATION

Special Thanks:

To my parents for being lifelong instructors of doing the right thing, for being my first teachers, and for instilling in me the belief that a good education is important and that anything is possible if you put your mind to it.

To the Journalism Department at Louisiana Tech University, for laying the foundation for me to have a successful career in journalism and subsequent career in public relations. They taught me to be a writer, and regardless of what I do each day, whether it's giving a keynote or teaching a training class, I know that it all comes back to my roots as a writer. I am a writer everyday.

To my professional colleagues, especially in the National Speakers Association, the International Association of Business Communicators and the Public Relations Society of America. Thank you for pushing me to always adopt best practices, to keep my skills sharp, and to be on the leading edge of whatever the next great thing is in the field of communications and professional speaking.

To Elizabeth and Gabrielle, my daughters, who are my daily inspiration and motivation to achieve more in order to provide for their needs. Your smiles warm my heart and your achievements make me proud.

To Cindy, my wife, who is always my partner in good times and in bad, and in sickness and in health. You are my rock. You make me a better person each day. Thank you for your patience and understanding as I travel around the world to do what I do. The best trips will always be the ones when I have you at my side.

I'm the luckiest man in the world because of the people who have touched my life. Thank you, thank you, thank you.

TABLE OF CONTENTS

FOREWORD

Life is good! Business is booming, your employees just landed another profitable client, as well as the cover story for the next Forbes magazine. It's Friday afternoon at 4:00pm, you've got a full weekend planned and a home soon to be full of guests... and then your phone rings. It's CNN's new reporter who needs a statement regarding the "situation" that just occurred at your business. Sound familiar? If you haven't encountered this type of PR emergency when you're the one on call, consider yourself lucky. Be prepared, however; no matter how big or small your company may be, and what the "situation" may end up being, it's only a matter of time before you get the call.

Since you are reading this book, you are already ahead of the "situation." In your hands is an easy to peruse, no-nonsense book on how to handle reporter calls professionally, and in a manner that can not only help you "find your way out of a mess," but can also help you look at any call as an opportunity. Mind you, it's the next best thing to hiring someone like Gerard Braud. He has a knack at helping even the media-queasiest executives feel confident about delivering their key messages. He was the first person I'd call when we hired a new officer to be media trained before we needed to count on them. At Best Buy, our employees are the key to our success. It's important to make sure they are well prepared, well trained, and an expert at what they do. If you can't hire Gerard for the up close & personal media training, read this book and keep it handy for those who can help you and your business.... and by all means read Lesson 9.

Susan Hoff
Chief Communications Officer, Retired
Best Buy Co., Inc.

HOW TO USE THIS BOOK

This book is intended to be a quick learning system and quick reference guide for anyone who has to be interviewed by the media. The book can be quickly read in its entirety, then placed in a briefcase or computer bag for future reference. For the busy executive on the road, this is a perfect book to read while waiting at the airport or flying to your next appointment. While the lessons do build in chronological order, much can be learned by simply jumping ahead to the lesson that interests you the most.

Finally, this book gives you great advice and lessons. However, as the book emphasizes, you are best prepared for a media interview when you combine the lessons in this book with actual role playing in a media training class. Please see the resources page in the rear of this book for more details on how to schedule a private media training class.

LESSON 1:
DON'T TALK TO THE MEDIA

This first lesson may seem counter intuitive, so let me explain what I mean. You don't want to talk to the media, but to the media's audience.

Ask yourself, who is that audience and how smart are they? The general rule is that the average person who watches TV news has a 6th grade education. And, the average person who reads a newspaper reads at an 8th grade reading level. Those listening to radio news fall into those same ranges.

So when you do a media interview, you need to be talking to those people and using words and language that those people understand.

Drop all the big words. You don't win any prizes for being multi-syllabic.

Can the corporate jargon. Synergistic win-win collaboration means nothing to anyone but you. And get rid of the government speak and axe the acronyms. Neither your audience nor the media should need to be a code talker to decipher what you are saying.

Think of it like this... If you were asked to speak at career day to a 6th grade class at your local school, what would you say? In fact, my assignment for you is to call a local school and ask to speak at the next career day. It's a great exercise.

OK, so the skeptics out there may disagree. Here are the things I hear from the skeptics:

- Well, I'll just tell the media what I know. It's their job to simplify it.
- I don't want to dumb it down.
- What will my peers think?
- My audience is different.

My answer is bull, more bull, definitely bull and absolutely bull. If you want the media to get it right then simplify the information for them. Do their job for them. Do the translation for <u>your</u> audience.

No one wants you to dumb it down and I'm not asking you to dumb it down. I want you to simplify it. There is a difference. I want you to be inclusive. I want you to respect what the audience may or may not already know. Be kind. Help them out.

As for what your peers will think, seldom will your peers be your audience when you do a media interview. Chances are your potential customers are your audience. Doctors should not use technical medical information but should use bedside patient language. Corporate people should not use corporate speak but customer speak.

New research also indicates that even people with college degrees and advanced degrees prefer to read at an 8th grade level. Information overload means they really want to be able to skim and quickly digest everything they have to read, whether it is a newspaper, e-mail, web site or memo.

You have a responsibility to communicate in a way that the media's audience will understand. You have a responsibility to communicate in a way that is easy for the media to understand, digest and repeat.

So our first rule is "don't talk to the media." If you'd like a reminder, send an e-mail to me asking that I send you one of my "Don't Talk to the Media" post cards. You can put it on your desk where you'll see it every day (my address is gerard@braudcommunications.com).

In our next lesson, we'll talk about the connection between profit and a media interview.

LESSON 2:
THE BIG IF

The Big IF is what I call my philosophy of media training.

I ask every executive that I media train this all important question: If you could attach a dollar to every word that comes out of your mouth, would you make money or lose money?

This is true for corporations that depend upon customers.

This is true for non-profits that depend upon donations.

This is true for government agencies that depend upon taxpayer and legislative approval for funding.

Say the wrong thing and your customers will buy elsewhere.

Say the wrong thing and your donations will dry up.

Say the wrong thing and funding to your government agency gets cut.

Say the wrong thing and lose your job. It is that serious.

Many executives are hesitant to carve out time in their schedule for media training. Why? Primarily because they think they are too busy. That translates into they are too busy doing things that help them or the organization make money (although, send them an invitation to a charity golf tournament and most will fit it into their schedule.).

Many people who do media interviews also let their egos get in the way. They are afraid to go through media training because they are afraid someone will see them mess up. It is for that very reason that I tell all of my media training students that at the end of class I insist they destroy the video tape used in our role playing interviews so that all of their mistakes stay in the training room.

The things I hear most often from executives who will not train are:

- I'll just wing it.
- I'll just be honest, shoot straight and tell them what I think.
- I don't want to sound rehearsed. I like to be spontaneous.

My answer to that is that if you wing it, you'll crash and burn.

As for honesty, I believe you should always be honest. The key to honesty is to choose every word carefully. For example, if we gathered a group of your biggest competitors in a room and asked you to unveil all the secrets to your business model and success, would you really tell them everything you know? Would you give them your playbook? It is a question of honesty after all. So if a reporter asks you the same question, will you tell them everything? They are going to print it and give it to your competitors.

As for being spontaneous, I spent 15 years in the media listening to people be spontaneous with me everyday. As they spoke, most days my general thought was, "I can't believe this idiot just said that to me on camera." By the time those comments were edited into my report and put on the evening news, most of those spontaneous, poorly worded comments were damaging to the spokesperson's reputation, which also has a negative impact upon the organization's revenue.

Was it fair for me to use the dumb, incriminating, negative things people said to me? Absolutely. After all, those people must have thought it was important because they said it to me. I'm just sharing their honesty with the public.

Let me also emphasize this. It's one thing to look stupid in the news report. But the damage does not stop with the damage you do to your personal or organizational reputation. Every time you damage your reputation you lose money. How much you lose depends upon how big of a gaff you make and the specific topic.

When you say something stupid that gets in print, on the radio or on TV, you also destroy your credibility with your employees. You also cause embarrassment to your employees and you potentially have a negative effect on their productivity; that will cost you money also.

So I ask the question again: If you could attach a dollar to every word you say, would you make money or lose money?

A well prepared, well rehearsed, well internalized message makes people want to do business with you, buy your products or support your cause.

As for not wanting to sound rehearsed, it is important to realize that the old adage about practice makes perfect is true.

Many people make the mistake of trying to memorize what they want to say. Memorizing means you only know the words in your head. The secret is to internalize what you want to say. Internalizing means you know it in your heart and you know it in your heart to be true.

In order to *internalize* your message, you first have to go through the process of learning it in your head before transferring it to your heart, then sending it from your heart to mouth.

If it is a lie, you cannot store the message in your heart and you will not be able to effectively verbalize it. So internalizing your message means that it is a well worded honest message.

My final tip on this topic is to treat every interview with the same importance that you treat every business deal. Before entering into a contract, countless hours are spent in preparation and negotiations. Why? Because it affects the bottom line. Well, the same due diligence and time needs to be put into preparing for a media interview. That means you need to schedule time to anticipate questions, prepare well worded answers, and to train and practice until you get every answer perfect every time. Then and only then should you do an interview with the media.

Every interview is as important as every business deal.

In our next lesson, we'll take a look at the wants, needs and desires of the media.

LESSON 3:
IT'S ABOUT ME

My wife often reminds me that it's "not about me." But she forgets that I come from a 15 year career as a journalist, where everything was about me.

Everyday it was <u>my</u> story; <u>my</u> interviews; <u>my</u> scoop.

Reporters have big egos. Accept it. You can't change it so don't even waste your time and energy.

To be successful in an interview, you have to know and understand the wants, needs and desires of a reporter. They include:

- I want a hot story.
- I want to be the lead story, which is the first story in the newscast or the first story on the front page.
- I want to build a positive reputation.
- I want to advance my career.
- I want to impress my boss.
- I want a raise.
- I want my TV station to have the best ratings.
- I want my newspaper to have a high readership.
- I want to be recognized as a good reporter by my peers.
- I want to win awards.

Do you see a trend here? I want, I want, I want...

Give reporters what they want, but give it to them on your terms. Take care of them and they'll take care of you.

Help them tell a great story and they will treat you right.

The best single tip I have for you in this category is to talk in great quotes. A quote is one of the single most important things a reporter needs for a story. Sure, facts are important. But when it comes time for the reporter to write the story, your quote makes or breaks the story.

Most spokespeople concentrate too much on trying to convey facts.

The anatomy of a TV news story is this: the reporter writes 1 or 2 sentences to set up the premise or "lead" for the story. The next 2 sentences are a quote, followed by a 2 sentence transition that sets up a second quote. Then the reporter wraps up the story with a summary. A newspaper story is similar, but 3 to 4 times longer.

When you speak in quotes you are actually writing part of the reporter's story. I'll bet you didn't realize that.

Anatomy of a TV News Story

Lead	Sound Bite	Transition	Sound Bite	Stand-up	Conclusion
:15	:15	:15	:15	:15	:15

Anatomy of a Newspaper Story

Lead	Quote	Transition	Quote	Details	Repeat
2 sentences	2 sentences	2 sentences	2 sentences	2-4 sentences	more sentences

Here is one other weird thing that reporters do that no other professional does. A reporter gives away a portion of their job each day to a complete amateur. Yep – a lawyer doesn't let an amateur try their case or write a contract; an accountant doesn't let an amateur do the math or balance the books; an engineer doesn't let an amateur run the chemical plant; a doctor doesn't let an amateur do surgery. But a reporter turns over a portion of their script – the quote – to you – an amateur. Doctors, lawyers, engineers, accountants, etc., are not professionally trained writers. Yet they are writing a portion of the reporter's story when they start talking in an interview. Some part of that interview will be quoted and that means you are writing a portion of the final script.

Great quotes are seldom spontaneous for the spokesperson. That is why they are best written by a professional writer and public relations expert. It is the spokesperson's responsibility to ask for help crafting quotes and then also their responsibility to go through media training and practice so the quotes are internalized, honest and sound unrehearsed.

In our next lesson we'll examine those age old responses from spokespeople who say, "the media took me out of context and they left my best stuff on the cutting room floor."

LESSON 4:
THEY TOOK ME OUT OF CONTEXT AND
THEY LEFT MY BEST STUFF ON THE CUTTING ROOM FLOOR

The 2 single biggest complaints I have heard from executives over the years, after they have done an interview, is that "the reporter took me out of context" or that "the reporter left my best stuff on the cutting room floor." (If you are young, the cutting room is where film was edited for TV news prior to the mid 1970's. Film that was not used in the story was thrown to the floor during editing.)

Here is the God's Honest Truth – First, if it was your best stuff it would be in the story. What you think is your best stuff and what the reporter thinks is your best stuff may be very different. But <u>no</u> reporter leaves your best stuff on the cutting room floor. Secondly, reporters never intentionally take anyone out of context. If you are taken out of context there must be a reason for it and I think I know why. Let's break it down –

In lesson 3, I emphasized the importance of talking in well worded, professionally written quotes. Why do we all know Neil Armstrong's quote, "That's one small step for man; one giant leap for mankind"? The reason we know it is because it is a well written quote from a professional writer which Armstrong practiced as part of his pre-flight training. It was not a spontaneous thought or ad lib by Neil Armstrong as he became the first man to set foot on the moon.

Your best stuff should be a well written, practiced quote. Hey, if it is good enough for Neil Armstrong, it should be good enough for you.

Unfortunately, spokespeople who refuse to go through media training are usually guilty of making some spontaneous, inflammatory statement that becomes the quote. Generally, they say something really dumb that they regret later. The problem is that once it is said, it's said. There is no taking it back. There is no do-over.

So my big rule for you in this category is that someone is going to edit what you say; it should be and must be you. Editing starts when the quote is written.

And remember this -- reporters all recognize a good quote. If you want proof, attend a news conference and watch the reporters as they take notes. It is like watching a ballet as all of the reporters raise their notebooks at the same time to write a quote or fact as the spokesperson says something important. Then all of them put their notebooks down together, then raise them all together again as they hear the next important quote or fact.

Let's now look at the issue of "they took me out of context."

Being taken out of context is usually the fault of the spokesperson. It is generally caused by the spokesperson being unclear, transposing important words, speaking in jargon or trying to give too many facts. That results in the reporter misunderstanding what the spokesperson meant. In short, something gets lost in translation.

How can you keep from being taken out of context?

Don't try to overload the reporter with facts. Reporters write in an inverted pyramid style. That means they start with a headline that is the synopsis of the story. Then they add the next broad general fact and so on. Seldom does the reporter get into great detail and an abundance of facts. So, don't get caught in the trap of trying to give too many facts.

Also, realize that the flaw of giving lots of facts and details is often a personality trait. Accountants, engineers, doctors and lawyers live in a world of details where numbers and facts must be precise. Hence, they want to be exact in what they say and they say too much; they give details beyond the reporter's comprehension. A print reporter is likely only writing a 12-20 sentence synopsis, a radio reporter is only writing 6-8 sentences and a TV reporter is only writing 10-12 sentences. Usually the miscommunication begins when the spokesperson may want to tell the details of "War and Peace," but the reporter is only looking for the CliffsNotes.

If you keep it simple you help the reporter write their story without miscommunications or misinterpretation and you won't be taken out of context. That's why in so many media training programs the trainer will ask the spokesperson to focus on just their 3 most important messages.

Next, forget the corporate and non-profit jargon, buzzwords and the government acronyms. Jargon, buzzwords and acronyms are speed bumps to comprehension. They are easily misunderstood by the reporter. The reporter then writes what they think they heard you say. However, if you were not clear, then the story will be wrong. It is your fault and not their fault.

Finally, before the interview is over, ask the reporter if they clearly understand all of the words you used. An embarrassed reporter may nod their head in agreement, yet be too embarrassed to ask you to define certain terms that you used.

In summary... Keep it simple.

In our next lesson we'll address bias in the media.

LESSON 5: THE MEDIA ARE BIASED

There is much debate about whether the media are biased, especially whether there is a liberal bias. If you truly want to explore that subject, I suggest you read the book *Bias,* by Bernard Goldberg.

It has been my experience over the years that much of what is perceived as bias is really the result of the following:

- Editors send reporters out of the door armed with only partial facts or rumors.
- The reporters and editors have misconceptions or misperceptions about you or your issues.
- A competitor or opponent of yours has approached the media and only told them half of the story.
- Ignorance by the reporter.

All four of the above result in the reporter calling you, asking for an interview, and asking you negative questions, putting you in a defensive posture.

Let's break it down.

Partial facts are usually the result of rumors and innuendos. We all share rumors every day. "Hey, you know what I heard today...?" In the newsroom, a reporter or editor turns that rumor into a research project and must confirm or refute it. "Hey Gerard, I heard a rumor today that... Why don't you go check it out?"

That rumor would become my assignment for the day. If there is a rumor that the mayor is on cocaine, then I try to prove that the mayor is using cocaine. If he is, it is a story. If he isn't, then there is no story. If the rumor is that the married congressman has a girlfriend, then I try to prove the congressman has a girlfriend. If it is true, I have a story. If I can't prove it, then there is no story.

You may not like it, but it is the nature of the business.

The next issue is very similar; it's the impact of a misconception or misperceptions. Often this is purely subjective. Perhaps you are proposing a new development, but something just seems shady. Then the news report may likely reflect a tone of skepticism. The reporter may even seek out a 3rd party who is willing to cast further doubt on your project or credibility.

On the issue of opponents -- I've watched many opponents make compelling cases and provide an enormous amount of supporting material and a hefty helping of innuendo. In the U.S., they're often called "opposition groups," while around the world they are called "NGOs," which stands for non-government organizations.

Usually the members of these groups are very passionate about a specific issue and those issues may be considered liberal issues. If a member of one of these groups makes a compelling case to a reporter, they could trigger a news report about you or your company. The reporter may come armed with reams of documentation supplied by the opponent, placing you in a defensive position. The resulting story could portray you in a very negative light.

And the final issue is ignorance by the reporter. Sometimes reporters just get the wrong idea about something and pursue it as a negative story. For example, most reporters look at steam belching from an industrial facility and think they are seeing pollution. Hence, they may do a story about industry polluting and fill the report with images of the stack belching what looks like smoke.

When you are faced with a situation like this, you need to apply all the tricks from lesson one, which includes explaining everything to them in simple terms the way you would explain it to a 6th grade class at career day.

Chances are the media are not "out to get you." But somebody else may be out to get you and they are letting the media do their dirty work.

In our next lesson we'll talk about how you can predict what questions a reporter will ask you in an interview.

LESSON 6:
I WONDER WHAT THE NEXT QUESTION WILL BE?

I want you to think for a moment about the last interview you did with a reporter. The reporter asks you a question then you start talking. Think very carefully now – what were you wondering the entire time you were answering the question?

In most cases, my media training students will confess that the entire time they were talking, they were thinking, "I wonder what the reporter is going to ask me next?"

Well here's a little confession – Most of the time while I was a reporter, the entire time people were answering my question I was wondering what I was going to ask them next.

This means that in most interviews, both people are distracted, wondering what the next question will be and therefore neither is really concentrating on what the current answer is.

Therein lies the biggest problem in most interviews and therefore the greatest opportunity.

Here is what you need to know about reporters to fully understand how the interview will go down. In most cases, the reporter has no written, prepared questions before the interview. And chances are, the reporter has not done an extensive amount of advanced research.

If you are dealing with an investigative reporter or a television network news magazine, you can expect the reporter has done more research and has some specific questions to ask. But in your average interview for your average story I would estimate that 80-90% of the time, the reporter is going to make up the questions on the spot when the interview begins.

The interview will start with "soft" questions, designed to help you relax and get into your comfort zone. As the interview progresses, the questions will become more direct and possibly more negative.

But here is the big secret – how you answer the current question will dictate what the next question is. Even more specifically, the words you use at the end of your answer will often be used by the reporter to craft the next question.

In other words, the reporter will mirror your language right back to you in the form of a question. For example, if my final words are, "…the challenges we'll face next year will eclipse the challenges we face this year…" what do you think the next question will be? The reporter will ask, "What are the challenges you expect to face next year?"

To test this theory, watch a TV news anchor talking to the reporter who is live on the scene of an event. The anchor will ask a question and the reporter will repeat part of the question back to the anchor as part of their answer.

Mary the Anchor: "Bob, it sure looks like a disaster zone out there…"

Bob the Reporter: "It sure is a disaster zone out here, Mary…"

I've developed a system for crafting answers that foreshadows the things that I want to talk about in an interview, followed by a "cliff hanger" or a sentence that creates some suspense. The trick is to always stop short of giving all of the details about something and to make the reporter want to know more. You want to <u>make</u> the reporter ask you a logical follow up question.

This technique makes life easy for the reporter because they never have to think very hard about their next question. You, therefore, are controlling the interview and the questions. The reporter is just following along.

I teach an entire workshop on crafting these "Kick-butt Key Messages." Unfortunately, time here doesn't permit me to teach the entire program. You would need a half day to truly learn the technique and system I use. But in the meantime, observe news anchors tossing questions to reporters on live locations and in your next interview try to create a few "cliff hangers" that will make the reporter ask you the logical follow up question that <u>you</u> want.

And finally, in lesson 3 we talked about creating quotes. In every interview you need to talk in sound bites and quotes. Often reporters keep asking questions because, while they may already have enough facts to write the story, they don't have a good enough quote to put into the story. And here is a big secret – the faster you give the reporter a good quote, the sooner the interview will end.

In our next lesson we'll explore the old myth that you should never get in a fight with someone who buys ink by the barrel.

LESSON 7:
NEVER GET IN A FIGHT WITH SOMEONE
WHO BUYS INK BY THE BARREL

I find it unbelievable that in the 21st century we still find executives who don't want to take on a reporter or news outlet that has wrongly damaged their reputation.

The traditional way of responding to a media outlet that makes a factual error is to ask the management for a retraction. But sometimes the issue is not always factual but a difference in your point of view. If a newspaper does a hatchet job on you, the correct way to respond is to always write a letter to the editor. The letter should be short and to the point, with about 200-400 words. In some cases, you may want to ask 3rd party supporters to also write short letters on your behalf.

Yet I still find executives who say, "We're not going to respond. Just let it die. You can't get in a fight with someone who buys ink by the barrel." That statement was wrong 50 years ago and it is even more wrong today.

In the past, a negative story may have run on TV or radio once or twice for 60-90 seconds, then it was gone. In the past, a negative story appeared in the newspaper for just one day, then the paper was thrown out, never to be seen again.

But the internet has changed all of that. Today, those negative stories live on in archives on the internet forever. Additionally, media websites are among the highest ranked websites on the internet because their information is deep, the site is constantly updated, and it is perceived by search engines as highly credible. The media sites are so highly ranked that if your organization or name is mentioned in a news report, the media website could come up as a higher ranked site on the internet than your own site.

What this means is that if I do an internet search for your name, or that of your organization, I may see and read the negative things written about you on a media website before I read the positive stuff about you on your own web site.

So what do you do?

Well, just as always, if it is a newspaper that has damaged your reputation, you should write a letter to the editor as I've outlined above. That letter to the editor now becomes part of the online archive linked to the story. That way, in the future, when people stumble across the story they will immediately find your point of view as well.

In the case of radio and TV, you should place your comments on the media outlet's blog on their website. Please be aware that other web users and opponents may verbally attack you and your comments once they are on the media outlet's blog. You need to be ready to clearly state your case.

Additionally, you may wish to place a response on your own website and blog. Blogs are highly valued by search engines and will help counter the negative comments from the original story.

Finally, don't take it personally. Your response is as important as a business decision, as we outlined in lesson 2. Hire professional PR writers to help if necessary. They will take the issue less personally and likely choose better words that may temper any anger you are feeling.

In our next lesson we'll explore why the facts don't matter.

LESSON 8:
THE FACTS DON'T MATTER

One day, as a joke in the newsroom, I uttered the phrase, "Don't let the facts get in the way of a good story." We all laughed. A colleague was pushing for a story to make the evening news, but there were lots of holes in the story and I (who in lesson 3 emphasized that it's all about me) wanted my story to be the lead story. I won and got the lead story. The colleague's story was killed.

Over the years we used the joke several times daily just to razz each other. But then we began to realize that way too much of what made the news at our TV station, and at those of our competitors, made the news, regardless of the facts. Ultimately, it was one of the reasons I left the news business after a great 15-year ride.

But let's be honest. How many news stories are filled with facts? The truth is, not a lot. Newspaper stories will always have more details than TV and radio news reports. But TV stories, especially, are driven by visual images. The example that I always use is that if the story is about a brown cow, I need video of a brown cow. If I have no video of a brown cow, I can't put the story on the evening news.

Another example I always use is the mixed metaphor that says, "If a tree falls in the woods and it is not on video, is it news?"

When I used to cover hurricanes in the '80s and '90s I was always upset when I didn't have video of something blowing away. I needed the visual on video to tell the story.

I laughed a few years ago when there was a news report about a landslide in Japan. A highway traffic camera captured trees sliding down the side of a hill. It was only news because there was dramatic video. Trust me, as a guy who has worked around the world and extensively in the Pacific rim, there are landslides all over the world every day. This one happened to be captured on video and therefore became news.

As I mentioned in lesson 4, a print reporter will likely write only a 12-20 sentence synopsis, a radio reporter is only writing 6-8 sentences and a TV reporter is only writing 10-12 sentences.

The average person tries to give way, way, way too many facts in a news interview. Take this comment with a grain of salt, but the reporter doesn't really care about you or the facts. Sure, they seem interested in you, but their report is more important to them personally than your facts.

A news report is a puzzle. Certain pieces must fit exactly together. In a TV report, quotes make up 1/3rd of the story. The lead and the conclusion together make up 1/3rd of the story. I don't want to burst your bubble, but can you guess how much room we have in the story for your facts? In a TV news report, that equals 4 sentences. In a print report, that equals 8-12 sentences.

If there is no room in the story for a bunch of facts, why would you spend so much time giving lots of facts to the reporter?

So, in conclusion for this lesson... don't let the facts get in the way of a good story.

In our next lesson we'll explore the media training myth about 3 key messages.

LESSON 9:
THE MYTH ABOUT 3 KEY MESSAGES

So, in the last lesson, we talked about not letting facts get in the way of a good story. The secret is to keep it simple.

When you go through media training (which I enjoy teaching more than anything in the world and I would still do every day even if I won a $200 million dollar lottery)... when you go through media training you are always taught the concept of identifying your "3 Key Messages." In other words, what are the 3 most important things you need to communicate during your interview with the reporter?

But what is a key message?

Is it a bullet point?

Is it a talking point?

Is it a set of words that incorporate more spin than truth?

Is it a set of verbatim words that incorporate both truth and quotes?

In my world, it is a set of verbatim words that incorporate both truth and quotes. But many media trainers teach only bullet points and talking points. I call this the myth about 3 key messages.

Let's put this in the context of a U.S. political candidate in a debate with his or her opponent. The moderator of the debate might ask a question such as, "Please give me your thoughts on education."

The candidate, whose strategist may have determined that the key messages should only be about energy, the economy and international relations, is left with nothing to say. Hence, the candidate will BS his or her way through 50 seconds of a 60 second answer, then conclude by saying, "education is important and you can get more details on my website."

That is such bull.

When you give a spokesperson or executive only bullet points and talking points for an interview, you give them license to ad lib. Have you ever seen anyone who can truly ad lib well? They are few and far between. The person who ad libs is doing what? They are winging it. What did we learn in Lesson 2? When you wing it you crash and burn.

In my world, you should start an interview with 3 key areas that you want to talk about. For each of those areas, you should have learned and internalized several pre-written sentences that are also very quotable sentences. Then, each of those 3 areas should have 3 key messages of their own, that are well written, internalized and quotable. And conceivably, each of those 3 key messages will have 3 more messages to go with them.

Think of your conversation as a large live oak tree like you see in the southern United States. Picture that tree with a huge, study trunk and 3 large branches. In my training programs, I teach the executives what I call my tree trunk message, which usually consists of 2 sentences that anchor the entire conversation. (Fig. 9.1) These are the first words out of your mouth when the reporter asks the first question. These first two sentences provide context for the conversation you are about to have. Both sentences must be quotable. The first sentence serves virtually as a headline that sums up your organization's vision, value, mission and belief. The second sentence points to the 3 key areas that the spokesperson is prepared to talk about. The second sentence begins the foreshadowing process that we talked about in lesson 6. It is this type of foreshadowing that will help the reporter develop his next question for you.

Next, I write 2 more sentences for each of those 3 large branches that grow from the tree trunk. Can you visualize this large oak with 3 large branches? The sentences must again be highly quotable. These sentences add a few more overarching facts and point to other important areas that you may want to talk about. Again, you are foreshadowing other areas that you are prepared to talk about.

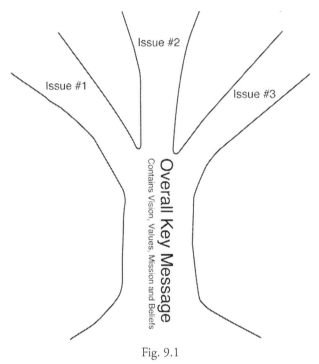

Fig. 9.1

Again, this is a technique that I usually take half a day to teach in my "Kick-Butt Key Messages" workshop. But if you can visualize a tree with a large trunk and 3 large branches, you begin to understand how the conversation grows. Then add 3 limbs to each of the large branches. Then add 3 twigs to each of the limbs. Then add 3 leaves to each of the twigs. Draw it out if necessary to fully visualize the tree. Ultimately, just as a tree sprouts limbs, twigs and leaves, your conversation needs to sprout additional sentences with slightly more detail.

In our visualization, the leaves represent great detail while the tree trunk and 3 branches symbolize very basic facts.

If you invest time to populate your tree with verbatim, quotable sentences that you internalize, your next interview will be the easiest interview ever.

Basically, your populated tree has created a full conversation and an interview should be a conversation. It should tell a story.

Additionally, our tree analogy has prepared us to tell our story in the inverted pyramid style – the same style reporters use when they write.

Is this easy? No.

Does it take preparation? Absolutely.

How much preparation? An interview is as important as any business deal. If you could attach a dollar to every word that comes out of your mouth, would you make money or lose money?

Bottom line – know what you want to say, know it verbatim, and be prepared to tell a story.

In our next lesson I'll ask you the question I ask often when I talk to people who use lots of jargon, corporate speak and acronyms. The question is, "What does that mean?"

LESSON 10: WHAT DOES THAT MEAN?

The question I ask most often these days is, "What does that mean?"

I'm relatively well educated. I'm well read. I travel the world, constantly teaching media relations and crisis communications.

But what bugs the ever living daylights out of me is hearing people speak in mumble jumble that they think means something, but it means nothing at all.

The mumble jumble is corporate speak, buzzwords, jargon and government acronyms.

I'm fortunate enough that people pay me an honorarium to speak at numerous conferences, corporate meetings and association meetings every month. I always make a point of listening to what other speakers say so I can incorporate their lessons into my presentation.

But many of the speakers fill their presentations with so many buzz words, jargon and mumble jumble that I find myself sitting in the audience asking, "What does that mean?" The speaker thinks they have said something profound, but they've really said nothing at all.

I hear things such as, "If we work in a customer centric capacity to increase productivity and to create a win-win situation for our partners in a collaborative fashion, then we can achieve our goals for the betterment of our strategic partners in the hopes of benefiting those with whom we do business?

What does that mean?

Were you trying to say put customers first?

What is a win-win situation? (with all due respect to Steven Covey)

What are examples of collaboration?

What are the goals?

Who are the strategic partners?

Please, spell it out. Please give me meaningful examples. Please give me tangible examples. Please give me anecdotes. Please communicate with real words. Please put some emotion into your communications. Please make the communications more visual by describing who and what you are talking about.

Let's go back to lesson one. Would those words work at career day with a 6th grade class? A friend of mine uses this test – if you were to say it to your grandparents at Thanksgiving dinner, would they know what you mean?

Let's touch on one other important point that I find in the politically correct world, especially among non-profit organizations. There is a propensity to say things in a way that will not offend the people that you serve. However, in the process of crafting your statement with sensitivity, you become so ambiguous that no one really knows what you are talking about, including, and sometimes most importantly, even the people they are trying to help. That's right; the people you are trying to help don't know what you mean, because the organization is being so sensitive and so politically correct.

If you keep changing the labels and the terminology out of sensitivity, then the audience, the reporter and the people you serve will be left asking, "What does that mean?" As we learned in lesson 4, that could lead to you accusing the reporter of taking you out of context. And as we learned in lesson 2, it affects your bottom line when you use terms that your audience cannot understand because of the politically correct ambiguity.

Consultants and trainers are also guilty of trying to coin clever phrases. A few years ago my wife, who works at a small private school, mailed out the class schedule for the fall semester. Her phone started ringing off the hook because, after years of promoting the school's top notch computer lab, computer classes were no longer listed on the class schedule. She told concerned parents she would check it out and get back to them. As it turns out, someone on the school staff had taken the term computer class off of the schedule and replaced it with the term "information literacy." Yes, it seems someone had gone to a summer workshop in which the trainer/consultant preached that "it's so much more than just knowing the mechanics of a computer, the internet and the programs – It's really about 'information literacy.'" What does that mean? It's a dumb term. Call it what it is. It's computer class.

If you'd like more examples from my "What Does that Mean?" file I have a great PDF that I'd be happy to share with you so you can share it with the offenders. It is available as a download at www.braudcasting.com

In our next lesson, we'll examine how people criticize the media for what is often referred to as interviewing people who have no teeth.

LESSON 11:
WHY DO THEY INTERVIEW PEOPLE WITH NO TEETH WHO LIVE IN A TRAILER
(WITH ALL DUE RESPECT TO TRAILER DWELLERS)

Let's be respectful here and realize that many poor people don't have either dental insurance or the ability to pay out of pocket for dental care. And let's realize that while hoping to someday fulfill the dream of home ownership, many people live in an affordable alternative – a mobile home.

Let's also recognize that many of these people are in lower income brackets and therefore also tend to live near industrial facilities where the more affluent members of society may work, but do not live.

With all of that out of the way, let me acknowledge that when I was a journalist, people would actually ask me, "how come reporters always interview people with no teeth who live in a trailer?"

The answer was, because when the industrial facility blew up, no one from the company would agree to an interview with us. The people living near the facility were the only eye witnesses and they were willing to speak.

If you work for a company that has a crisis, you have the responsibility to provide a spokesperson as soon as the media arrives. Usually the media will be on site within 30 minutes to an hour, depending upon the crisis. And as more media outlets become dependent upon web based audiences, their need for news is even more immediate.

Reporters need facts and quotes and they are going to get them from somewhere. It is their job to get interviews and their job is on the line if they do not deliver.

If you don't give the information to the reporter, the reporter will go get it from someone else and that someone else will likely not represent your point of view.

And as the age of Social Media and web based tools expands, more and more media outlets are depending upon digital photos and video taken by eyewitnesses. A simple cell phone is capable of doing an enormous amount of reputational damage by providing the media with pictures and video.

So what do you do?

First, you need to establish policy and practices that insure you have a spokesperson ready to respond at a moment's notice.

Secondly, you need to have a crisis communications plan that contains a vast array of pre-written statements designed to address all of the many crises your organization could face.

With those two things, a spokesperson should be able to pull a pre-written template out of the crisis communications plan and walk out to the media to deliver that statement. It also allows your organization to post the template to the web, e-mail it to the media, employees and other key audiences.

Even if you only have partial facts, your organization still needs to make a statement. And it is critical that the statement is delivered by a person and not just issued on paper or via the web. The human element is critical in gaining the trust of the media, employees and other key audiences. A written statement is simply a cold cluster of words.

In my world, the spokesperson should be able to deliver the statement live within one hour or less. It should never be longer than an hour and hopefully much sooner than an hour.

One of the biggest delays in issuing statements is the lengthy process of waiting for executives and lawyers to approve a statement. This delay should be eliminated with the pre-written statements. The statements should be pre-approved by executives and the legal department so that the public relations or communications department can issue statements quickly.

Creating such a template is a timely process that I take organizations through when I help them write their crisis communications plan. The process is too lengthy to discuss here. But certain portions of the template must be fill-in-the-blank, and the communications department must be authorized to fill in the blanks with information such as time, date, and other critical facts. Executives and lawyers need to establish a trusting relationship with the communications department so that they help speed up the process rather than hinder and delay the communications process.

When you follow these simple steps, you begin to manipulate the media because you are meeting their wants, needs and desires. You also become their friend. The more you can provide the media with information, the less need they have to interview an ill informed eyewitness who is thrilled to have their 15 minutes of fame. The more you can occupy the media's time, the less time they have to spend interviewing people with no teeth who live in a trailer.

In our next lesson we will discuss whether or not you can pass the cynic test.

LESSON 12:
PASSING THE CYNIC TEST

Reporters are among the biggest cynics in the world. They doubt everything you tell them and you have to prove everything to them. This is especially true if you are trying to promote a good news story.

I have found over the years that reporters are quick to believe something negative about your organization and slow to believe your positive side of the story. We discussed some of these issues in lesson 5 when we talked about opposition groups and NGOs.

Reporters are always wondering what you are trying to hide and what you are not telling them.

We walk a thin line sometimes, because while I am in favor of always telling the truth, I do agree that there are times when you need to practice the sin of omission. At no time are you obligated to go to confession with a reporter just as you are not obligated to tell a competitor all of your secrets, as we discussed in lesson 2.

As a Catholic, I learned early the virtues of going to Confession. But while we are taught that when you go to Confession in the Church you receive absolution and forgiveness, I can assure you that if you go to confession with a reporter you will go to hell.

I know because there were many days when people went to confession with me, only to end up on the front page of the paper the next morning or leading the newscast that evening.

I have two rules as it relates to passing the cynic test. The first rule is to write well worded key messages using simple language that everyone can understand. Those key messages need to be void of any flowery words that would be construed as heavy on PR (public relations) or full of BS (the stuff that you find in a pasture near a cow). PR and BS stink a mile away and cause reporters to become very cynical.

My second rule is what I call the "3 Bucket Rule." Imagine three buckets sitting in a row. (Fig. 12.1) In bucket number one I would put all of the positive key messages that I need to say in an interview. Bucket number 2 would be filled with well worded key messages about a vast number of negative things the reporter may ask me about. I label bucket number 2 as things I will only talk about if asked. Bucket number 3 will be the smallest bucket and it will contain things that I cannot talk about. Such issues might be confidential employee information, confidential corporate information, or private medical information. Various laws by various governments may prohibit you from discussing these private details.

| Things We Must Say | Things We Will Only Talk About if Asked | Things We Cannot Discuss |

Fig. 12.1

As you share the key messages from bucket number one you should be telling a logical story using the reporter's own inverted pyramid style. The facts should fall logically into place. At the end of each key message you should create a "cliff hanger," as we discussed in lesson 6, designed to make the reporter ask you a logical follow up question. This natural progression will make the reporter feel as though you are being open and honest with them, because you are.

Should you be asked something that is in bucket number 2, you will follow the same procedure of giving a well worded, pre-written key message using the inverted pyramid style. The facts should fall logically into place. At the end of each key message you should create a "cliff hanger" that helps the reporter craft a logical question that you can answer. In the process, you should be guiding the reporter back to more of the positive key messages from bucket number one.

In media training classes, we teach the technique of block, bridge and hook. This technique traditionally teaches that when you are asked a negative question, you block the negative by bridging to something positive and hooking the reporter with new information. The technique is designed to distract the reporter with perhaps something that is more appealing and has more wow.

The danger with the block, bridge and hook technique is that the redirect, or bridge, is so overt that you never answer the reporter's question and that makes the reporter even more cynical and skeptical. It may actually anger the reporter and cause them to become hostile.

The approach that I teach is to answer the question with a well worded key message, which serves as a "block" because it gives enough information to answer the question without exposing more vulnerabilities. That key message from bucket number 2 is then followed with a bridge back to more positive information, which is then followed by a fact, statistic, story or example that might contain more wow than the line of questioning the reporter was previously pursuing.

The block, bridge and hook is a difficult task to teach without actually role playing and it is difficult for me to do true justice to it in this forum. To truly learn the technique you should really schedule a training class with extensive on-camera role playing.

And remember, as we learned in lesson 8, the faster you get to a quote, the faster the interview will end. Make sure your key messages are full of quotes.

In our next lesson we'll go deeper into crisis communications and examine how those cynical reporters quickly cast a vote of no confidence in you when you don't respond in a timely manner.

LESSON 13:
THE VOTE OF CONFIDENCE OR NO CONFIDENCE

In lesson 11 we discussed the fact that when there is an industrial accident and a spokesperson does not appear in a timely manner, reporters often go looking for facts and quotes from other people, such as the ones with no teeth who live in trailers.

Something else happens, which also ties into lesson 5 on bias.

When a reporter arrives on the scene of a disaster or crisis they immediately began sizing up the situation and deciding whether they have confidence in you or no confidence. I often liken it to the European parliaments that will cast a vote of confidence or no confidence in the Prime Minister.

If disaster strikes and no one is around to tell the reporter what is going on, the reporter will cast a vote of "no confidence" in you.

The result is ugly. They question whether you have your act together. They question whether the situation is potentially more dangerous than it actually is. I remember thinking as a reporter, standing outside of a burning chemical plant, "These people don't have their act together. This is going to get uglier before it gets better. We're all going to die."

As a result, my cynic filter, as discussed in lesson 12, would be set off and bias would begin to creep into my report. In a live report you might hear the cynicism in the tone of my voice or hear a tone that sounds sarcastic.

Additionally, the words I put in my script would become slightly more inflammatory.

If I was forced to go for an extended period of time without official information from the company involved, then anger would begin to creep in. I had editors and managers yelling at me wanting me to deliver the facts, and no one from the company was actually helping me. Remember, in lesson 3, we discussed the fact that it is about me. And when you don't help me that is also when I would head out to the local neighborhood to begin asking neighbors what happened, whether they were afraid and what their opinions were of the company.

This is when I would usually hear comments such as, "They have explosions over there all the time," "There's no telling what's in the air," "I'm afraid to live here," "My eyes are watering and my throat is scratchy," and my all time favorite quote, "It blowed up real good." (Yes, I actually had someone tell me that on camera one day.)

Sometimes the no confidence factor went even higher when a security guard would show up and tell us to turn off our TV camera, even when we were standing legally on public property. I'd always make sure we showed the security guard on the evening news because his actions or words clearly said this company had something to hide. Once, the owner of a company even tried to run me over with his car.

The ugliness of no confidence continues, because when the official spokesperson finally comes forward, the reporter's question will be far more negative, sarcastic and downright lethal.

As a corporate coach and trainer I understand that perhaps no one came out to speak to me when I was a reporter because everyone in the facility was busy fighting the fire. But let's be honest. I don't care. One person needs to be designated as spokesperson. It is part of your corporate responsibility to have a well trained and well qualified spokesperson, just as it is your corporate responsibility to have a well trained and well qualified team of emergency responders to fight the fire.

On the other hand, if I arrived on the scene of a burning factory and was met promptly by a courteous spokesperson with only the most basic facts, my confidence in the company went up astronomically. I immediately thought, "Wow, these people have their act together." That would make me cut them some slack and grant them some forgiveness. The questions to the spokesperson were much kinder and gentler. The tone of my voice in the live report was more fair. Sarcasm was removed from my delivery. Additionally, because I had facts and quotes from an official source, I had less need to knock on doors in the neighboring community to ask ill informed eye witnesses what they saw, heard and feared.

So in summary, be ready to have your spokesperson on the scene quickly with a well worded statement as part of your crisis communications plan, as we discussed in lesson 11.

In our next lesson we'll look at how to deal with reporters who want you to speculate.

LESSON 14:
REPORTERS LIKE TO SPECULATE

What's the worst that could happen? How much worse could it get? But what if... ? Oh, those great "what if" questions.

Reporters love the what if question. Why?

Well, reporters love a great story and sometimes the story doesn't materialize the way they hoped it would. Remember all the lessons on selfishness that we discussed in lesson 3? Well, all of that comes to fruition and is personified by the what if question.

Such questions indicate that the reporter is as disappointed as a 4-year-old who was hoping you would stop to buy them ice cream, but you didn't.

Beware of reporters who ask you to speculate, because you are heading into very dangerous territory. If you do speculate, you've made the story bigger than what it is.

The most important phrase you can use when addressing such questions is to say, "I couldn't speculate on that, but what I can tell you is..."

Another variation of that answer is to say, "It would be inappropriate for me to speculate on that, but what I can tell you is..."

Such answers apply the block, bridge and hook technique we discussed in lesson 12. In this case you block their speculations right up front with the phrase, "It would be inappropriate for me to speculate...," then the phrase, "but what I can tell you is..." should bridge to redirect the reporter back to one of your key messages and one of the facts that you have previously confirmed. Ideally, you should create an additional hook that keeps the reporter from asking another speculative question as a follow up. But the most important thing that you are doing is immediately putting an end to the speculation and sticking to the facts.

Akin to this is when a reporter will ask you to speak for someone else. The proper response should be, "I can't speak for them, but what I can tell you is..." You then use the same block, bridge and hook techniques we discussed previously.

One more lesson we should also address here is how to handle the reporter that misstates certain key facts in their question.

It has been my experience that most spokespeople try to gingerly work their way back to a key message and then correct facts without ever clearly telling the reporter they are wrong. Well my friends, that seldom works.

If a reporter misstates a fact in their question you have permission to stop them dead in their tracks if necessary and say, "I'm sorry, but you misstated a key fact in your question." At that time you should give them the correct fact. Another variation is to use the phrase, "I can't agree with the premise of your questions."

Over the years many spokespeople have confessed to me that they are afraid that such an approach could be perceived by the reporter as hostile. I personally think you can do it without being hostile. In fact, I have found that the dynamics of the interview or news conference will change in your favor because the reporter sees that you are in charge and that you are holding them accountable. The reporter will not only choose their words more carefully in the remainder of the interview, but they will also choose their words more carefully when writing their script.

Ultimately, you must realize that you are in charge of the interview. Don't relinquish control to the reporter.

In our next lesson we'll examine how a spokesperson can get the most out of a media training class.

LESSON 15:
HOW TO STRUCTURE MEDIA TRAINING

One of the most difficult challenges I have in my job as a media trainer is to get executives to carve out time in their schedule for training. As mentioned in lesson 2, some don't see the financial benefit. An even greater percentage are afraid of whatever embarrassment they may go through during the training.

Admittedly, it is difficult for high powered people to intentionally put themselves in a vulnerable position. But media training requires an executive to exercise a little humility and to recognize that training is a great time to learn a new skill or perfect an old skill.

So here are some suggestions, whether you are the executive who needs to be trained or whether it's your job to convince an executive that they need media training.

Everyone needs to understand up front that the day needs to be fun and that they need to be ready to laugh at themselves and their mistakes. Making mistakes is part of learning, i.e., you learn from your mistakes.

Just the same, I try to create a safety zone for the student. If the person being trained is the CEO I prefer that we are the only two people in the room. At a minimum we can expect the class to take 4 hours. And as a sign of good faith, I always promise to destroy the video tape that we used to record mock interviews during the training.

If it is basic media training to familiarize an executive with the concept of media interviews, I'll generally conduct 3 interviews during the course of the training. The first interview is a simple baseline interview. It lets me gauge the executive's natural skills and personality type. I'll determine quickly if the student is prone to give too many details, for example. I'll also test their ability to stay on topic or whether they are easily distracted and get off topic easily.

The interview is recorded on video so it can be played back, evaluated and critiqued, even if you are practicing for a print interview.

I'll then introduce the concept of using key messages to stay on topic and control the interview; then we will do a second interview on camera, followed by another evaluation.

My third interview begins to introduce negative questions and is designed to teach the concept of blocking a negative question by bridging back to one of the key messages and then hooking the reporter with new information.

I conclude the training with four things. First, I let the student destroy the video tape as promised; secondly, I give the student instructions that in order to truly master the skill they must begin using key messages every day in ordinary conversations. Thirdly, I tell them they must role play with someone before every interview. Even if you only have 5 minutes, you need to get your head in the game and your mouth in gear. Finally, I let them know that media training is not a one time event in life, but something that requires practice and more training. Hopefully, top executives understand the concept of having personal success and life coaches. I suggest an ongoing approach to media training with a refresher course taught ever 6-12 months.

For groups of vice presidents, managers and directors, the choice is yours as to whether you offer them a private 4 hour training, or whether you combine them into small groups for a full day of training. It is my personal preference to have no more than 4 people in a full day training program. When you add additional people you may need to add a second video camera and interviewer in order to complete all 3 role playing interviews in the allotted time.

In some cases, clients will ask for a training program to familiarize large groups with media training and the do's and don'ts of media interviews. Such classes are possible. I've conducted programs with hundreds of people in the room. You can teach them all of the same lessons you would in a small media training class, but you are obviously unable to do personal role playing interviews with everyone. Generally, I'll bring a volunteer to the stage to show everyone how an interview should be conducted. Then I ask the audience members to partner with the person next to them to conduct an interview. The audience members each take a turn to ask questions and to answer questions. Then I lead them through the process of giving each other an evaluation.

Finally, one way to get hesitant executives to train is to incorporate presentation training into the program. Many of the skills used to make a good presentation are some of the same skills used in an interview.

I always remind my students that Michael Jordan did not become the best basketball player of his day after a single practice, nor did Tiger Woods become a great golfer after taking a class at a Putt-Putt course. Likewise, to truly master the skill of being interviewed, you have to practice on a regular basis and find a coach and trainer who is a good match for your organization.

In our next lesson we will look at the big difference a little practice makes.

LESSON 16:
PRACTICE, EVEN IF YOU ONLY HAVE 5 MINUTES

In our last lesson we talked about how to structure a media training class and how I always tell the executives I train that they must practice before every interview, even if they only have 5 minutes. I'd like to expand on that and explain why this is so important.

I was training an executive who is the CEO of a Fortune 100 company. As I often do, I asked to see some video tape of his previous interviews so I could know more about the person I was training and his natural strengths and weaknesses.

A video tape arrived at my office, featuring the CEO conducting a news conference at a major trade show for his industry. It was downright painful to watch. This executive was rambling extensively. There was little or no emotion in his voice. He seemed to be reading a long laundry list of accomplishments and corporate goals. For all practical purposes, the news conference had no focus.

At the start of our training session I pulled out the video tape and suggested we watch it.

"Oh you don't want to watch that," he said. "I was terrible in that. Trust me... I did that presentation 3 times that day. The third time I was great."

So I asked him to break down who was in the audience for each of the 3 presentations. As it turns out the first time he did it, the audience was composed of stock analysts. The second news conference was held for mainstream media. The third news conference was held for trade publications.

As he explained who his audiences were, he quickly realized that his worst performance was for his most critical audience. He failed to perform at his best for stock analysts who can potentially have the greatest positive or negative impact on his company. If you think back to lesson 2 you'll remember my admonition – If you could attach a dollar to every word that you say, would you make money or lose money?

I asked if he practiced the news conference at all on the day before. He told me no, because he didn't have time. I then pointed out to him that if he had practiced 3 times the day before, he would have done a great job in front of his most financially critical audience.

Practice makes perfect, and even if you have only a few minutes before heading out to talk to the media, you need to practice and role play with a colleague or coach.

What we want to say, what we think we're going to say and what actually comes out of our mouths when we start talking are all very different.

A "back stage" practice changes all of that. It only requires someone to ask you a few questions, starting with the very basics. You really want to make sure you can nail your opening lines and command the audience's attention. You want to make sure you can eliminate any of the stutters, stumbles and misspeaks that often happen in the first sentence.

I find that if a spokesperson can have 2 good practice sessions, their third time – which is the real event – will go smoothly.

Obviously, in an ideal world, I would like to see the spokesperson practice for more than just 5 minutes, but 5 minutes is better than nothing.

So often, spokespeople fail to spend any time in preparation, especially if it is a good news story. As often happens, they attempt to "wing it." As a result, their good news story may get little or no coverage because they failed to deliver a great opening statement and then failed to really clearly state their key messages in great quotes. Generally, the spokesperson who does not practice in advance will have a monotone delivery and, like my CEO friend, will stand at the podium and offer a long laundry list with very little focus.

The bottom line is, you need to always carve out time to practice, because what you say will affect your organization's bottom line.

In our next lesson, we'll take a closer look at good news stories and how you can get the media to say Wow!

LESSON 17:
WHAT MAKES THE MEDIA SAY WOW! -COMMIT NEWS

As a reporter, I generally hated going to a news conference or a media event that was about good news. It's not that I'm opposed to covering good news, it's just that generally the spokespeople were poorly prepared and the organizers were completely oblivious of the wants, needs and desires of the media.

If you call a news conference or organize a media event, you'd better be prepared to commit news. When someone commits murder, it is usually a pre-meditated act. Well, good news needs to be pre-meditated as well. You need to commit news.

The litmus test we use in the newsroom is to first ask, "Who cares?" Actually, in most newsrooms everyone curses like sailors, so how we actually phrase the "who cares?" statement is a lot harsher. To pass the litmus test, the answer needs to be that a large portion of our viewing, reading or listening audience cares. That's how news is determined.

Too many good news events fail to meet that basic test of affecting or bettering the lives of a vast number of people in your community. A ribbon cutting is not news. Expanding your facility is not news. The anniversary of when your organization was founded is generally not news. Yet every day, the newsroom is filled with news releases asking the media to cover such events.

It is not news if the event is self-centered and all about how good your organization is. To be news, you must explain how it is good for that broad audience. To quote my wife – it's not about you. It needs to be about the audience at home watching TV, reading the newspaper, listening to the radio or following the story on the web.

For something to be news, you also have to make the media say Wow! That means you need to knock their socks off with a catchy hook, have good quotes and good visuals. Often adding wow means you have good timing and you are able to link your issue or event to something else important in the news. For example, holding a blood drive on a clear sunny day is likely not news, but holding a blood drive to help the victims of a crisis is news. Holding a food drive on a clear, sunny day is likely not news, but holding a food drive to help victims of a major natural disaster is.

I teach a workshop called, "What Makes the Media Say Wow!" My favorite case study in that program is one for a litter clean-up event that I was asked to handle Public Relations for. The event is called Beach Sweep. It is an annual event that organizes thousands of volunteers to fan out along the Louisiana coast to pick up trash that has washed up on the beaches. While the event initially got lots of media attention, after covering the story for several years, media attention had died off.

To add wow I added controversy. In our state legislature there was a huge battle between a group of recreational fishermen and members of the commercial fishing industry. Fishing in Louisiana has a huge economic impact because more seafood is caught in our coastal waters than in any of the lower 48 states. With that said, I called the leaders of the 2 feuding groups and asked if they would both lay their differences aside for one day. I further asked them to call on all of their members to help pick up trash in the coastal waters as they went fishing on Beach Sweep Saturday. They both agreed. I then asked both leaders to act as spokespeople at a media event. These feuding parties standing side by side helped to create the wow I needed.

Next, I needed the event to be visual, so I held it at a boat launch where the fishermen could take reporters out by boat to see the trash problem first hand.

Finally, I provided just enough media training for both spokespeople to teach each a handful of good quotes and how to deflect any probing questions about their ongoing battle in the state legislature. The best quote was crafted by simply asking the fishermen to hold a landing net and to demonstrate how it could be used to pick up trash, while saying, "This landing net is the best tool a fisherman can have this Saturday because you can land a trophy fish and you can use it to pick up trash." It was what I call a show-and-tell quote. Four TV stations used the same quote, as did one radio station and every newspaper.

I knew going into the event that every reporter was really covering the story hoping to get greater insight on the legislative fight. When asked about the fight, the spokespeople were taught to say, "We'll talk about that another day. Today we're here to talk about something that is important to every fisherman, which is to clean up the environment."

Hence, we committed news, told a story that impacted the economy, every fisherman and everyone who uses the waterways and beaches. That means we had all the pieces of a perfect story. And, to add icing to the cake, every reporter thanked us for making the story so easy to cover because we met their wants, needs and desires by giving them a story with a great hook, great quotes and great visuals.

In summary – be ready to commit news and don't try to make the news about you; make it about your audience.

In our next lesson, we'll talk more about how to prepare, media train and practice for an interview being conducted by an investigative reporter.

LESSON 18:
PRACTICING FOR THE BIG NEGATIVE NEWS STORY

So far we've discussed what an ordinary media training program includes and we've discussed the need to practice before every interview. But if you are being interviewed about a negative issue by an investigative reporter or a major publication or network news magazine, you need more than your average media training and quick practice session. You need to prepare as though you are going to war.

There are two main steps you need to take:

• Your Public Relations or communications team needs to become the investigative reporter

• You need to train until you know the answer to every question.

Let me explain what I mean.

When I'm asked to prepare someone for such an interview, we usually have one to two weeks to prepare. Major publications and networks often spend weeks and months working on a story.

Preparation includes numerous phone calls with the reporter or producer to find out exactly what their story is about and what they want to know. Reporters are very coy and really don't want to tell you too much about the story. Ideally, they want to catch you off guard because they think you will be more honest if they catch you unprepared. In most cases reporters are very vague when they ask you a question.

If you are a retailer, for example, the reporter may tell you they are doing a story about computers, when really the story centers on allegations of questionable behavior by your computer sales team. If you are with a non-profit, they may tell you the story is about donations and how the money is used, when the real story is about high executive compensation and justifying a 6 figure salary funded by donations. If you are with a government agency, the reporter may tell you the story is about helping tax payers, when the real story is about a long list of tax payer complaints.

The first rule you should apply is to look in the mirror and to realize that the good Lord gave you 2 ears and 1 mouth and that you should use them in that proportion. In other words, you should be asking the reporters more questions than you answer. You need to learn to ask them probing questions about the possible report, then stop talking and start listening. Listen for not just what they say, but what they don't say. You must become an expert in reading between the lines.

Among the questions you should ask are:

- Can you tell me a little about the genesis of the story?
- Is the story about something that we do well or something that you think we could do better?
- Ultimately, what do you want your audience to take away from the story?
- Who else have you talked to?
- What have those people told you so far?

I have a total of 3 pages of questions like these that I provide privately to my clients. It would be a disservice to print them here and tip our hand to the media.

After you ask the question, sit back and listen. Too many people think they need to do all the talking when dealing with a reporter. In this case, you want the reporter to do all the talking. And on the topic of talking, be aware that even though you may be doing advance work for the primary spokesperson, everything you say can be used in the final news report.

After doing exhaustive questioning of the reporter, the next step is for you to write the story the way you think the reporter would write the story at this very moment in time, based on what they said and didn't say. Be brutally honest, cynical and sarcastic as you write the story. Next, share the story with your executive team to get their attention and commitment to do whatever it takes to fight the good fight, including more research by a team of people, designating a spokesperson, and a full commitment from the spokesperson to clear his or her calendar for media training.

With the executive team you should then pick apart the story to separate fact from fiction and perception from reality. Quickly identify where the reporter is off base in his or her assumptions. Identify the source of the story and what you know about the person or persons who may have given the story idea to the reporter, as well as what you know about the other people the reporter has already interviewed.

Next, develop a long list of questions that you think the reporter might ask. Do not be kind in crafting these questions. Make them very direct.

After that, you'll need to research the true answers to each question, gather background material to support your position, then begin writing answers to every question. The answers must all be quotable and written in the key message tree style that I described in lesson 9.

Media training for this type of interview may take 1 or 2 days. Generally, such training will include a 45 minute role playing interview recorded on video, followed by an extensive critique and then more long interviews. This goes on non-stop until we've flushed out every question and until the spokesperson has perfected every answer. Remember, this is serious stuff that could affect your business and your bottom line.

Often, I run into cynics who say you can't possibly know every question you'll be asked, nor can you know all the answers. I beg to differ with them. I have and you can. In fact, the greatest compliment I get from clients after their interview is, "Gerard, you nailed it."

You can nail it too.

If you get in a jam, you can always send an e-mail to me and track me down at www.BraudCommunications.com

In our next lesson we'll examine media training for a desk side visit.

LESSON 19:
PREPARING FOR A DESK SIDE VISIT

If you are a big organization, occasionally a reporter from a major media outlet will call and ask for permission to do a "desk side visit."

Be careful. These can be deadly.

A desk side visit is when a reporter wants to come by the office, not to write a particular story, but to visit with key executives and get to know them. Most often the reporter will be with a major newspaper or magazine and usually the reporter has recently been assigned to cover all stories related to your company, non-profit, agency or business sector.

While it is true that the reporter wants to get to know you, the entire time they are with you they are taking notes that will be filed away and used as story ideas at a later time.

The big danger occurs when PR people get excited that a reporter wants to visit and when the executives let their guard down and enter into too many friendly, candid conversations with the reporter.

Take a guess what everyone needs to do before participating in a desk side visit? You guessed it... they need to go through media training.

I have seen an enormous number of executives go to confession with reporters during desk side visits, only to see their own words come back to haunt them months later in a report they didn't even know the reporter was writing. Do you remember what I said about going to confession in lesson 12? I said if you go to confession with a reporter you'll go straight to hell.

So what should media training look like for a desk side visit?

First, the communications team needs to haul out all of the company's key messages and dust them off to make sure they are current. Ideally, the communications team should have a deep library of key messages with more written each time a new issue arises.

Next, you need to segregate your key messages according to the 3 bucket rule that we discussed in lesson 12. That means you need to identify the key messages that you must say, which is bucket number 1. Then in bucket number 2 you will find the answers, or key messages, that you will use only if you are asked about certain issues. Then in bucket number 3 you will have things that you cannot talk about at all.

Because people have an overwhelming compulsion to be honest, many people immediately begin telling reporters negative things that are usually kept in bucket number 2. I call this "opening the door." Once you open the door, you've invited the reporter to enter and ask you many more questions. You have in essence opened Pandora's Box and closing it is nearly impossible.

Many executives assume that everything in a desk side visit is "off the record." It is not. Everything is on the record. And for the sake of clarity, never ever think that anything is off the record with a reporter. In fact, if a reporter ever invites you to speak off the record, you should refuse to do so. What you say to the reporter will always get traced back to you.

Likewise, be aware of reporters who ask you to speak on "background." This means they want you to tell them facts, but they promise not to quote you or attribute the facts to you. Again, the people you are talking about will be able to figure out that it was you who was trashing them.

When done correctly, a desk side visit can be a great way to create a positive perception about you and your company. In lesson 13 we talked about passing the vote of confidence or no confidence with a reporter. A desk side visit is a great way to pass the test of confidence.

Finally, if the desk side visit goes well, key executives may want to call the reporter from time to time to share tips about trends in your industry. Their purpose should never be to have the reporter write about you or your organization, but to establish yourself as a trusted expert and source. Your goal is also to establish a true relationship with a reporter. That's why, after all, they call it media relations.

Ultimately, that relationship will pay off in the future and make it much harder for the reporter to write scathing or negative stories about you or your organization. There is a lot to be said for relationships.

In summary, a desk side visit could be your worst nightmare or it could turn out to be your best friend.

In our next lesson we'll examine how you can best internalize all those key messages we've been talking about.

LESSON 20:
THE SECRET TO INTERNALIZING KEY MESSAGES

In the early stages of media training, many students are skeptical about the concept of key messages. Accepting key messages and using key messages effectively takes time and practice.

As I mentioned in lesson 15, in most media training classes I first conduct a baseline interview, then I introduce the concept of key messages to the student, then I conduct a second interview to give them an opportunity to test drive a set of key messages that we have agreed upon.

After the second interview I always ask whether the second interview was easier or harder than the first. Usually 50% of my students think the interview is easier once they are given key messages while 50% think the second interview is harder when they have to remember key messages.

And as I mentioned in lesson 2, many people have difficulty with key messages because they try to memorize them. Remember, the goal is to internalize them. That means you learn them first in your head and over time, you grow to know them in your heart.

But how do you successfully internalize a series of key messages?

It begins when you start using all of your media training techniques and key messages every day. Sure, the class is called media training, but the skill set you learn should serve you well in presentations, when talking with employees, when talking with friends at a party, etc.

To begin with, work with a good writer to craft your key messages and make sure the key messages are written to match the way you speak. The key message needs to be in your voice using the kinds of words you would use, provided those words are not jargon. As we've mentioned before, if you are guilty of using jargon you'll have to cure yourself of that habit and the key messages may help.

But when I say put the key messages in your voice, I really mean that the sentences need to be structured to fit your speech pattern. Some people have difficulty pronouncing certain words. I, for example, have difficulty saying the word, "particularly." It is due in part to the speech impediment I had as a child. So I replace "particularly" with the word "especially."

Next, make sure the key messages are factually true. If there is the least bit of exaggeration or the slightest falsehood, you will trip over your words every time.

Once you have 2-3 key messages that you like, start using them every day in as many conversations as you can with as many different people. You need to essentially test drive the key messages the way you would test drive a car before you buy it.

Try this little test – Use the same key message 3 times a day with 3 different people each day for 3 weeks. By the end of three weeks, you will actually hear someone saying almost your exact words either to a colleague or back to you. What is amazing is that they will say it with confidence as though it is their own original thought. They may say it to you without ever realizing that they first heard it from you.

This point is further proven if we go back to our previous discussions about jargon. If the CEO constantly uses a phrase such as "customer centric," eventually all of the vice presidents will use the term, followed by all of the managers and directors. I worked for a major retailer as a vice president for a while. Within the first few days on the job I was overwhelmed by how fast jargon was transferred through the ranks. Your good key messages can be transferred through the ranks as well.

As you master the first few key messages, learn a few more and use them daily until they are internalized.

You'll notice that the first few times you attempt to interject the key messages into a conversation it may seem awkward. That is to be expected. But with each passing day, those key messages will begin to sound more conversational. Ultimately, that is your goal – to be able to use your key messages in a very conversational tone when you are talking to the media.

In our next lesson we'll examine the secret to a great interview and a great answer.

LESSON 21:
THE SECRET TO HANDLING NEGATIVE QUESTIONS

Most questions from most reporters are negative. News in general tends to be negative because it is usually about serious change or a disaster. I wish news wasn't negative, but I spent 15 years in the business trying to change that and couldn't. Then I've spent every year since 1994 trying to change it and I haven't made any progress.

With that said, I'm going to teach you the secret to answering a negative question. Let me go through the various steps first and then I'll explain each step.

You must:
- Listen to how the question is phrased.
- Ask yourself, is it a negative question?
- If so, realize you are not obligated to directly answer the negative question.
- Determine if the negative question can be phrased in a more positive manner.
- If it can, mentally ask yourself the positive question.
- Then, answer the question using a positive answer that responds to the positive question.

Of course, the time you have to do this is a nanosecond. But much like internalizing key messages is done through daily repetition, this skill set must also be practiced in daily conversation.

Let's break it down using an actual case study. In the late 1990's, a chemical company wanted to build a $700 million dollar facility in the industrial corridor along the Mississippi River about 40 miles upstream from New Orleans.

Ten years earlier, as a reporter, I covered a Greenpeace anti-pollution campaign along the river. Greenpeace nicknamed the area, "Cancer Alley." During a 2 week period of protesting, they convinced many people that cancer rates in the area were high and that the cancer was caused by chemical plants.

Scientific proof, however, indicated that cancer rates in the area were no higher than anywhere else in the world. However, mortality rates, especially from lung cancer, were high. That was because smoking rates were high, especially among the poor, who had no health insurance and were generally diagnosed with cancer after it was very advanced.

With that background, imagine the task of trying to build a new chemical plant in "cancer alley." Despite the jobs it would create and the economic impact, opposition groups were quick to allege that if built, the chemical plant would be a cancer causing polluter.

The turning point in this story came in a news interview where a television reporter asked the company spokesman, "Will this plant pollute?" His answer was, "Well, yes. We have permits from the state of Louisiana to produce caustic chlorine, EDC, VCM and PVC and those permits are essentially a license to pollute."

There are so many sins committed in this one quote, but let's stay on task and examine the question first.

Was the question negative? Yes.

What was the question behind the question? It was, "when you build this chemical plant, will it pollute and kill everyone with cancer?"

The spokesperson essentially said yes, the company will kill everyone with

74

cancer and that they had a license to kill.

Could there be a positive version to this same negative question? Sure, a more positive question would have been, "the people in the community are afraid your chemical plant will cause cancer. What assurances can you give them that you can operate in a safe manner?"

Do you see the difference between that question and the original question? Do you see how both questions are essentially asking the same thing?

The proper positive answer should have been, "In order for us to receive permits from the state and federal government, we must promise to be protective of human health and the environment. Let me tell you how we plan to do that..."

In addition to not answering the question in a positive manner, the spokesperson committed a whole host of sins. The sad thing about the original answer is the spokesperson was attempting to be honest, but in the end he was actually telling more of a lie than he was telling the truth. He was honest to a fault. Everything we do as humans causes pollution, from driving our car to flushing the toilet. And while there are always some emissions from chemical plants, much of the $700 million dollar price tag would be for pollution controls.

Additionally, because the spokesman's personality type was geared toward being a details person, he began listing the chemicals the company would make by name. To the average person in the audience with a 6th grade education, it was frightening jargon, equal to telling the audience he would be making "ethyl methyl death."

I'm going to guess the spokesperson did not practice before the interview. What's sad is I know he went through media training. I was not his trainer but I observed the class as one of the pioneers of media training worked with him. And remember my admonition from Lesson 16 that you should practice before every interview, even if you only have 5 minutes. If he had practiced for just 5 minutes before the interview, he likely would never have uttered those words to that reporter.

Finally, I am sure the spokesman did not attach a dollar to every word that came out of his mouth, because the $700 million dollar plant was never built and his quote was one of the main reasons.

To learn how to answer negative questions in a positive manner, you have to practice this skill daily as you practice your key messages.

In our next lesson we'll examine the role passion plays in media relations.

LESSON 22:
THE POWER OF PASSION

Few things are as underestimated in a media interview as the passion a spokesperson conveys.

In lesson 8 we talked about why the facts don't matter and how to create great quotes. If you learn to combine great quotes with passion you not only insure your quote gets used in a news story, but you can also dominate and control the direction of the news story.

Too often in the world of spin, "truthiness" quotes are developed that spokespeople memorize, rather than internalize. Hence the spokesperson sounds stiff and rehearsed when they deliver the quote.

A quote that is internalized and delivered with believability and passion gets used in a news story every time.

The best role model that I have for the power of passion is to study the behavior and media tactics of protesters and activist groups. One activist can say more in 4 seconds than all the facts a detail-oriented person can say in four hours.

The example that comes to mind most for me is the night I was covering a public hearing in which a multinational company wanted to build a chemical plant in a rural industrial community.

In this community, a vigilant group of environmental activists was working to convince the community that the proposed chemical plant would belch out so much pollution that it would essentially kill everyone with cancer. And although many residents believed the activist, an ever larger number of people believed that the plastics plant would bring much needed jobs to the rural area and help boost the area's tax base.

A public hearing was held in a rural courthouse and began with testimony by engineers from the company and environmental experts representing the state's department of environmental quality.

For several hours, engineers and scientists presented data on why the plant could be built and operated safely. It was excruciatingly painful to sit there for hours listening to the monotone drones of these experts as they moved through their boring PowerPoint slides.

Several hours into this hearing it was time for me, the reporter, to exit the courthouse, head out to my live truck and begin editing my story for the 10 p.m. news. I knew it was going to be a difficult story to write because I really didn't have any good quotes.

As my photographer and I began to gather our equipment and head to the door, a member of Greenpeace came rushing up to me. He said, "Gerard, you can't leave yet, we haven't had a chance to speak."

I assured him that I would tell both sides of the story and that I was willing to interview him or another representative of the opposition if they would just step outside of the hearing room with me.

"Just give us 5 more minutes," he pleaded.

Curious, I agreed to stay in the hearing room 5 more minutes.

As the engineer at the podium continued to drone on in monotone fashion, the activist stood, walked to the podium, delivered a thundering fist pounding to the podium and shouted, "This hearing is a sham and we are out of here!" With that, all of the opponents stood up and walked out of the hearing room. Wow!

With that, I had my quote to finish telling the story. In just 4 seconds, the activist said more than the official corporate and government experts said in several hours. All of those technical facts did not matter.

The quote from the activist summed up all of the frustration of the people they represented. Most of all, they passionately conveyed their beliefs. Although the scientists, engineers and experts may have high belief in the facts they presented, they were unable to present them with any passion. And while the protestors could be challenged on whether the hearing was really a sham, they successfully summed up and encapsulated their feelings.

The lesson here is that when you create those great quotes, internalize them, then add emotion and passion, to make them stand out and become memorable. When you do, you take control of not only the quote, but of the entire story.

In our next lesson we'll discuss ways to select the right spokesperson for your organization.

LESSON 23:
SELECTING THE RIGHT SPOKESPERSON

Picking the right spokesperson really depends upon the situation.

Many organizations tend to have two extremes in selecting spokespeople. Some organizations always send out their top Public Relations person while other organizations insist that only the CEO speak.

I endorse neither of these approaches as perfect and will suggest that sometimes the top PR person is a great choice and likewise in some cases the CEO is a great choice. But in many cases, neither of these people is a good choice.

In fact, if you think back to lesson 12, in which we talk about passing the cynic test, many reporters cynically will think that the Public Relations spokesperson will be too polished, slick and rehearsed, and is therefore serving as a buffer to protect executives who are afraid to talk and who are vulnerable to difficult questions. Conversely, if the cynics see the CEO out front as the spokesperson for certain events, they will assume that the event is more serious because the CEO is having to handle the situation.

As a reporter, I generally wanted to talk to the person closest to the story or issue I was covering. If a hospital has a new procedure to announce, I'd rather speak to a front line doctor than either the PR person or the CEO. If the news report is about a non-profit agency, the best spokesperson for the story might likely be a volunteer. If a company is accused of wrong doing, I'd like to interview the manager who is closet to the issue at hand. If there is a fire and explosion, I'd rather speak to an eye witness or line supervisor.

The closer you can get the reporter to the person closest to the issue or event, the happier they will be.

Of course, this means that when it comes to media training, you need to use the same principle that a great sports team uses. You must train lots of people and build bench strength.

Training deep means managing budgets and calendars such that you can do both primary training and refresher training on a regular budget. Usually, budgeting time and funds is proportionate to the size of your organization. In proposing deep training and budgeting, just remember that the value of a single news story can easily pay for a single media training session. In fact, in most cases, the relative ad value of a single news story is 3 to 9 times greater than the cost of a media training class.

As an example, a 30-second TV commercial during a newscast may cost $4,000 to $5,000, which might also be the cost of a single media training class. However, according to the rules of relative ad value, a 30 second TV news story is considered 3 times more believable than a 30 second advertisement; hence the relative ad value of a 30 second news story could be $12,000 to $15,000. Most news stories run 90 seconds, which could increase the relative ad value of a single TV news story to $36,000 to $45,000 dollars or more. To take it one step further, most towns have one newspaper, 3-5 television stations and multiple news radio stations. Hence, the relative ad value of a news event could easily be worth $300,000 or more, depending upon which city you live in and the price of a 30 second commercial. More modern measurement methods can be even more precise in measuring relative ad value because they calculate the positive and negative nature of the story. The bottom line is that you can easily justify investing funds to train multiple spokespeople based on the positive financial impact it may have. Remember our rule about, "If you could attach a dollar to every word you say, would you make money or lose money."

Hence, develop bench strength so you can have a large number of spokespeople to send forth and not just the head of PR or the CEO.

As for using the PR person, in Don Henley's song, "Dirty Laundry," he speaks of the bubble headed bleach blonde news anchor who comes on at 5 p.m. and how she can tell you about the plane crash with a gleam in her eye. Well the same is true of many PR spokespeople, which makes them not my choice on many occasions as spokespeople. Regardless of whether news is good or bad, some spokespeople are able to stand before reporters and maintain a bubbly persona as though all is well, even when it isn't. Their answers are often glib, superficial and poorly rehearsed. I hate that and so do most reporters and that is why many times I don't want a PR person to be the spokesperson.

At the same time, many CEOs attempt to be too serious, attempt to communicate way too many details and generally look like the world's biggest grump. I hate spokespeople like that.

The one time when I always want the PR person and the CEO ready to both act as spokespeople is when I write a crisis communications plan for an organization. I generally ask that the PR spokesperson and CEO both be included as spokespeople, along with a host of other executives.

Generally, in the first hour of a crisis, when information is still limited and most executives are busy managing the crisis at hand, I suggest that the PR spokesperson read what I describe as the "First Critical Statement." This document lays out the very basics of what is known until more details are available.

Generally, I follow the initial statement one hour later with a more detailed statement delivered by a manager who has more expertise and knowledge about the subject at hand. This is one of the reasons why mid-level executives need to be media trained.

Many companies will have sent out their CEO by this point to serve as the point person and lead spokesperson. I do not agree with this approach because I would prefer for the CEO to be leading the crisis team during the crisis. Furthermore, if a company uses a CEO as their spokesperson and the CEO misspeaks, who will come behind the CEO and clean things up if the CEO makes a mistake? Generally, I save the CEO to be the final spokesperson when the crisis is over. It both allows the CEO to clean up after any misstatements by middle managers and it allows the CEO to be portrayed as a leader who was managing the crisis.

Words are important, but you also send signals to the media by whom you select as your spokesperson. Choose wisely.

In our next lesson we'll discuss the do's and don'ts of a news conference.

LESSON 24:
DEATH BY NEWS CONFERENCE

Many reporters fear what I often call "death by news conference."

In lesson 17 we discussed the concept of committing news as a premeditated act. Reporters hate to cover news conferences for two main reasons. The first reason is because usually there are way too many spokespeople saying little if anything newsworthy, and secondly, because the location and setup are so poorly managed that it makes for a bad visual setting, especially for television.

Over the years I've witnessed three main approaches to news conferences. There is the news conference held in a conference room or pressroom; there is the news conference held outside under a tent; and then there is the news conference that I would describe as a show and tell event.

I like show and tell events the most. I hate outside under a tent events. The conference room or pressroom events vary.

What I like best about the show and tell events is that they are more visual. In lesson 17, I describe a media event that was held at a boat launch. The spokespeople did dockside interviews; then we put the spokespeople in boats with reporters, where the spokespeople were trained to deliver key quotes while in the boat and especially while on camera.

When planning a show and tell event, location and logistics are critical. And because these events may be outside, you need to consider weather forecasts and what your contingency plans are if you are sacked by inclement weather. Some show and tell events may be inside a factory or distribution facility. In these locations, sound and lighting may become problematic. If it is too noisy, reporters may not be able to hear the spokesperson and the background noise will be problematic for both radio and television crews trying to record audio. If the facility is dimly lit, has too much florescent lighting or a mix of both ceiling lighting and sunlight through doors and windows, photographers for television and print may have difficulty getting the images they need without adding their own complicated lighting to the mix.

My suggestion is that when planning a show and tell event, hire both audio and lighting experts to assist with the planning to make sure you meet the needs of news crews.

Under a tent events tend to follow ground breakings. A ground breaking is not news, yet many executives continue to think it is news. Usually the ground breaking is preceded or followed by a news conference under a white tent, in which the top executive serves as key spokesperson and master of ceremonies, and includes a thank you to every person under the sun (or under the tent). Then the executive turns the microphone over to an army of politicians who will do anything to get on camera. To add insult to injury, usually the tent shades the spokespeople and the daylight behind the spokespeople creates what photographers describe as a back lighting nightmare. Bright sunlight behind a spokesperson makes their face look dark. It is nearly impossible to add enough light to compensate for the bright sunlight. The problem gets even worse when the spokesperson has dark skin.

A few other notes about these ground breaking events. Most are really geared toward an internal audience of close associates who need to receive a thank you. That is not news and don't ever believe the media will include that in the news. Additionally, know that many reporters go to these events only because they need to ask a politician a question about another issue they are covering. That politician can often overshadow your event, and in many cases, will create a negative association that you should avoid.

As we move inside to the pressroom or conference room event, we face two extremes. One extreme is the blank wall seen behind the spokesperson, and the other extreme is the attempt to place logos either on the lectern (podium) or behind the speaker. Logos are designed to create greater awareness of your organization and brand. As a rule, when there is bad news to discuss, you do not want your logo seen anywhere. Conversely, when there is good news to share, the best option is to have a series of small logos on a wall size, non-reflective banner behind the spokesperson. Professional sports teams usually do this well, combining their logo with that of a corporate sponsor. Of course, before sponsoring any organization and splashing your logo behind a spokesperson, you should consider whether you really want to be strategically associated with that organization. If the team wins, you win. If the team loses, do you lose by association?

Government agencies tend to fall into a unique situation with their briefing rooms. The White House and Pentagon are good models to follow, with a blue curtain behind the spokesperson and a lectern logo.

When hosting a full-blown news conference, consider hiring an audiovisual company to provide professional lighting and audio. Professional lighting will keep the media from having to set up their own lights, which can be very harsh and make the spokesperson look bad. Professional audio means that one microphone can be placed on the lectern, with a single audio cable running to a multi-box where the television and radio crews will set up. Each news crew then takes their audio from the multi-box, eliminating the need for news crews to place their microphones, microphone stands and massive microphone logos on the speaker's lectern. When a lectern is crowded with microphones, three things happen: often the speaker has no place for his or her notes; the speaker attempts to adjust one microphone, causing an avalanche of falling microphones; or as the first news crew gets bored, they attempt to remove their microphone while the spokesperson is still speaking, breaking the spokesperson's concentration.

So, to recap – commit news, make the event visual and consider the needs of the media when it comes to location, sound and lighting.

In our next lesson, we'll discuss Social Media Training and how the internet should affect your behavior.

LESSON 25:
SOCIAL MEDIA TRAINING

The internet, the media on the internet, and the proliferation of self-ordained pundits on the internet, has forever changed the world. So has the proliferation of gadgets that let us rapidly post pictures, comments and video to the web. The ability for the global community to post online comments in countless ways and forums makes the world even more frightening for those trying to manage their reputation. For the sake of discussion here, when I use the term social media, I'm talking about all postings to the internet that allow your reputation to be improved or destroyed, as well as the gadgets that make it all possible.

There are three ways you can get hurt in the world of social media. The first is when your public actions are photographed or video taped, then posted to the web. The second is when your reputation is attacked on social sites and blogs, and the third is when you willingly participate in on-line discussions and do a poor job communicating.

One of my all time favorite videos, posted to the web, is of a county commissioner being hounded by a television reporter. When asked after a public meeting to justify the delay in opening a new county juvenile justice center, the commissioner asks the reporter, "Elliot, do you know that Jesus loves you?" The commissioner then dodges every one of the reporter's subsequent questions by trying to engage in a discussion about why the reporter should accept Jesus as his personal savior. Regardless of your religious beliefs, the answer is inappropriate because it is not germane to the news report, and by repeating a variation of it as the answer to every question, it only makes the official look more like he is guilty of hiding something.

Prior to the advent of social media tools such as MySpace.com, Facebook. com and YouTube.com, such buffoonery would have been seen once or twice on the local evening news, the commissioner would have become the butt of some brief local mockery and embarrassment, but within a few days it would all pass. But in the age of social media, millions of people around the world are able to watch the video and laugh at its absurdity on a daily basis. Some will post a link to their own website, or forward a link via e-mails to friends. This is what viral and social media is all about. This video lives forever on the world wide web and so does the commissioner's embarrassment, mockery and humiliation, as people perpetually forward the video to their network of real friends and online acquaintances.

Situations like this are one of the reasons you should consider Social Media Training.

Social Media Training is a program I pioneered to teach communicators and executives the realities and how their reputations can be damaged by public actions that are either voluntarily or involuntarily captured, and posted to the web.

More than a few reputations and careers have been destroyed because of what someone says in a presentation to what is perceived as a friendly group. Inevitably, an audience member records the speech or presentation, then either posts a portion of it to the web or gives it directly to the media. Cloaked with an audience of perceived friends, speakers often "cross the line" by their comments, only to face humiliation, embarrassment, and in many cases a long list of apologies and even the loss of their jobs because they thought their comments were made in private and off the record. If you are hosting a social media training class, you may wish to combine it with a presentation skills class.

Social Media Training is also needed before communicators and executives voluntarily attempt to participate in online communities. This is true whether one is responding to a posting made by someone else, or whether you are the one posting to a personal or corporate blog for your organization.

A case in point is a random blog entry I found one day as I prepared to teach a social media seminar. The blog entry was from a top executive from General Motors. The blog entry, posted on an official GM site, featured a photo of the executive. The guy in the photo looked like he was delivering an angry rant on stage at a corporate meeting. His blog entry, likewise, took an angry, rant style with a tone that personified, "I know better than you."

His comment was a reply to a blog posting critical of GM's poor gasoline mileage in its Sports Utility Vehicles. Because of how the executive worded his rather pompous response, many more participants in the blog criticized his parsed words and reply, which reflected the official corporate line.

In short, the executive's poor choice of words was like throwing gasoline on a small fire, turning it into a bigger fire. It didn't need to be that way.

Executives need to think carefully before they participate in social media and corporate communicators need to think carefully before asking or allowing executives to actively participate in social media.

There are a few basic things communicators and executives should consider in the world of social media:

1. Are you good with traditional media? If you are not good with traditional media, what makes you think you can handle social media?

2. How do you behave in public? Do you realize that every public moment of your life is potentially being photographed or recorded?

Your public behavior, what you do and say, who you associate with, and where you are seen in public, can all be posted to the web for the entire world to see.

My basic rules for social media are this:

1) Every rule of media training applies to social media. Every word and how those words are phrased will be carefully scrutinized.

2) Edit what you say constantly to avoid having your comments taken out of context.

3) The rule of ethics is to ask whether your behavior in private is the same as the way you would behave if people were watching you. Congruency of behavior is important.

4) Before jumping into an online blog type discussion, you need to be prepared to use key messages and make sure those key messages have been run through the cynic filter. Bloggers are cynical and brutal.

5) Sometimes the best response to a blog posting is to ask a question. Rather than attacking a blogger for their point of view, simply ask them to further explain their point of view. Sometimes a blogger will back down as they are unable to defend their position. Sometimes other bloggers will come to your rescue with responses that match your point of view.

6) Orwell predicted that by 1984 Big Brother would be watching everything you do. Orwell was off by 20 years, because by 2004 the ability for everything you do to be watched had become a reality. Big Brother is now everyone else in the global society.

In our next lesson, we'll return to the more traditional setting of a news conference and look at your appearance in a news conference.

LESSON 26:
LOOKS ARE IMPORTANT

Looks are important. With just three lessons left to go, I would be remiss not to cover some important basics, such as how to dress for a news conference.

Dress for men has always been easier than dress for women in the world of media. That's because men's fashions tend to remain basic, such as a coat and tie. About the only thing that changes much is the width of jacket lapels and the width of a tie.

Women, on the other hand, constantly face changing trends in clothing, ranging from sleeve types, to skirt lengths, to neckline styles. All of that is further complicated by shoe styles, hair styles and make-up styles.

As a basic place to begin, if you are in a formal news conference setting, traditional business attire is best. For men that is a business suit with neck tie. For women it is a traditional women's business blazer with business skirt or business trousers. Both men and women should consider basic colors such as black, charcoal gray and navy blue.

What you wear affects you in two respects. In one respect, you have to consider how the audience perceives you based on your appearance. In another respect, you have to consider how you photograph and whether your wardrobe cooperates with cameras.

From the perception of the audience, consider that while some women look great in a red suit, some audiences may perceive red as the sign of someone who is power hungry. While certain women's clothing may be trendy and acceptable in a social setting, in a business setting it may be perceived as too provocative. Women are likely to face greater challenges in this arena than men.

From the perspective of being photographed, many photographers complain that white shirts beneath a jacket make it difficult for them to compensate for the lighting on your face. This is less true today than in the past. As a rule, I think that especially for men, a white shirt is great under a business suit. Men have greater leeway with a white shirt than women do because it is broken up with a neck tie. Photographers often advise that a light blue shirt is often best for photography. From a lighting perspective it makes their job easier, but a blue shirt isn't always as professional looking as a white shirt.

Excessively bright colors, flowery fabrics and fabrics with intricate patterns should always be avoided. They may look great in the mirror, but they look especially bad on television. Such designs tend to glow or create what is called a "moray" or "zebra" effect on television, which becomes a distraction to viewers. Soon the viewer is paying more attention to your glowing wardrobe than they are to your words. I have to leave many of my favorite neckties home when I'm going to be interviewed for television, because they look good in the mirror, but look lousy on camera.

And as for television, standing to be interviewed on television is less of a wardrobe challenge than sitting. While sitting in a news studio you are likely to be seen from your head to your toes. For men that means making sure your shoes are shined and that your socks fully cover your legs. Men should not have a gap of leg showing between the top of their sock and where their pant hem starts. Large men especially need to make sure their suit fits well. Too many men put on weight and don't buy a new suit. This especially becomes obvious when their jacket doesn't fit well when they sit. As you practice and media train the day before your interview, you should review your clothing and how it looks on camera.

Women on camera should select a conservative shoe that is not too trendy. Most women on television select to wear a skirt rather than pants. Selecting a skirt means you need to consider where the hem line rides as you sit. You also need to consider whether you have attractive legs on camera, as they are part of your image. Exposed veins and bumps and bruises become a visual distraction, detracting from your words. As fashion trends vary, hosiery may or may not be in style. However, on camera, hosiery is the equivalent to make-up for the legs. Just as foundation and powder can cover skin blemishes on your face, hosiery can cover skin blemishes on your legs. Bare legs, much like bald heads, shine. The shine of bare skin is a distraction.

In considering these tips for women, keep in mind that television news anchors are increasingly breaking these trends, wearing trendy shoes, trendy dresses with little or no sleeves and often no hose. Some look downright silly and amateurish. Some can get by, for example, without wearing hosiery because they are still in the 20's and the skin on their legs has not yet betrayed them, as it often does to women beyond the age of 29.

For news events held outside of a news studio or a news conference room, a good rule to follow is to dress for the occasion and location. If you are in a factory, dress as a factory worker might. If you are volunteering at an outdoor charity event, a polo style short sleeve shirt or an appropriate long sleeve shirt with khakis may be appropriate. Both men and women should refrain from wearing shorts at such events. Likewise, don't wear hats when being interviewed or photographed because the hat brim often shades a portion of your face while leaving another portion in bright sunlight. Such a lighting contrast is especially hard for photographers to deal with.

As a final thought to appearance, yes, it is true that both men and women should wear make-up if you are being interviewed for television. This is especially true if you are in a television studio with harsh lighting. You'll notice that the news anchors are wearing a ton of make-up. The concept of make-up is often embarrassing to men, but you need to get over it and do it. When in doubt, hire a make-up artist who knows how to do television make-up. Keep in mind there is a big difference between general make-up that a woman may wear daily and how make-up is applied for men and women in a television studio. You may want to go the extra length and test out the make-up during your media training prior to your actual interview.

If you are outside and on television, a little press powder goes a long way to eliminate shine from oily skin. Balding men face an even greater challenge both in the studio and outside in the sun as the skin on their expanding forehead shines.

So in conclusion, in this lesson I've likely insulted both balding men and women with varicose veins. Sorry, I mean no offense. I'm just an old truth teller trying to offer you the most professional guidance possible.

In our next lesson, we'll examine body language.

LESSON 27:
BODY LANGUAGE

What you don't say is often as important or more important than what you do say when you are talking to a reporter. How you stand, how you act, how you fidget, how you move, how you stutter, how you sit, and where you look, all say a lot about you.

The easiest thing for a reporter to determine in an interview is that you are nervous. When I started my professional journalism career at the age of 21, I was five-feet-six-and-a-half-inches tall and 124 pounds soaking wet. I did not consider myself intimidating in the least. So why is it that learned people, such as doctors, lawyers, engineers and elected officials got so nervous? Why did they fidget so much? Why did they sweat on their brow line and on their upper lip?

Actions such as sweating are harder to control because they are a result of nervousness. However, if you follow all of the advice in this book, if you hire a good media training coach and if you practice on a regular basis, then your confidence will go up and your nervousness will go down.

Folding and crossing your arms across your chest in an interview is almost always a sign that you are hiding something. If you are crossing your arms because you are cold, a better alternative is to wear warmer clothing. Sales people have long known that a customer with crossed arms will not buy anything from them. In the world of journalism, crossed arms means you are closed off to the premise of the reporter's question and that you likely are not going to volunteer any information. Your body language may cause the reporter to probe even deeper because they can tell you are trying to hide something. If you are on television, the audience at home will also see this body language and may judge you harshly or relish in your discomfort. Many at home will sense that the reporter has "gotcha."

Your eyes are the proverbial window to your soul. I suggest that in daily life you get in the habit of looking people directly in the eye and maintaining an appropriate level of honest eye contact. Traditionally, we're taught that looking someone in the eye is a sign of honesty. Conversely, someone with high anxiety caused by not telling the truth usually has difficulty looking another person in the eye. You've likely heard people called "shifty-eyed." When your eyes shift from side to side it is an obvious sign of anxiety, discomfort, and begins to make the journalist think that you have something to hide. Behavior like this is a perfect example of why role playing with a video camera is so important during media training. You may shift your eyes all the time and never realize it until you see yourself on camera. Reviewing your interview on camera in media training lets you observe the behavior, then lets you work to correct the behavior.

Whether you look up or down and whether you look left or right also says a lot about you and what you are verbalizing, including whether you are "making it up" as you go.

If a right handed person looks up to the right while answering a question, they are generally being creative in crafting their answer and it may be perceived as a lie. If that same right handed person looks up and to their left when answering your question, it is generally perceived that they are recalling actual facts and telling the truth. Looking up is generally associated with questions about things that actually happened, things you saw or people you know.

Looking to the side has some of the same perceptions and generally applies to questions about sounds and things you have heard. Looking down to the left and right is a great deal less about telling a lie and more about feelings and recalling things such as a smell, touch or taste.

A left handed person performs these acts in the opposite direction of a right handed person. One of the classic case studies is former President Bill Clinton, who is left handed. As he made his infamous statement, "I did not have sex with that woman, Miss Lewinsky," he looked up and to the left, an indication that this lefty was a liar.

Other body language for lying includes touching your face, the tip of your nose, rubbing your eyes and covering your mouth. Essentially, these are all telltale signs that you are trying to hide something and hide, perhaps, behind your hand. Covering your mouth, for example, subtly says you don't want me to see you tell a lie.

How you sit tells us a lot as well. As a rule, never sit in a chair that rocks and swivels. If you do, when you become nervous or uncomfortable, you will likely rock or swivel.

Never do an interview while sitting behind your desk. This is usually a place that is too comfortable and very intimate to you. As a result, you may speak perhaps too bluntly and openly because this is your comfort zone. You need to be honest, but being behind your desk may cause you to let your guard down. Instead of sitting behind your desk, pick two chairs in front of your desk.

Your posture while sitting says a lot. If you cup your hands behind your head, as well as if you lean back while doing this, it indicates that you perhaps feel superior to the person interviewing you. Akin to this, slouching in a chair during an interview could be an indication that you are cavalier, arrogant or feel superior to the interviewer. Many people who are described as "cocky" sit slouched or leaned back in their chairs. During my days on television, we affectionately called these people "cigar smokers" because they looked like the fat-cat, cigar smoking corporate executive made infamous in the black and white movies of the 1940s.

The position of your legs while you sit also says a lot. Women and men tend to have different sitting postures. Women who have been through some degree of etiquette training have been taught to place their feet on the floor and to cross one ankle behind the other. (Fig. 27.1) This is always a polished look.

Most women, when crossing their legs, cross at the knee. The most common way women cross their legs might be called a scissors cross or inverted V cross, with the left foot pointed right and the right leg pointed left. (Fig. 27.2) From the knee, a woman's feet spread like an inverted letter V. This cross is also generally accepted, but when nervous, most women begin to twist the ankle of the foot that is suspended above the floor. Some may even swing the suspended portion of the leg from their knee to their foot. The more nervous a woman is, the more the leg takes on the appearance of kicking.

Some women cross their legs at the knee, then wrap the upper foot behind their calf. (Fig. 27.3) This is a certain sign of being timid, embarrassed or lacking self-confidence. This is never an acceptable posture.

Fig. 27.1

Fig. 27.2

Fig. 27.3

Also, when crossing their legs, women must also consider whether they are wearing pants or a skirt. If a skirt is worn, then the woman must also determine whether she is sending a message of sex appeal or sexiness. Some actresses and news anchors intentionally wear short skirts and sit in a posture designed to exude sex appeal. In the world of television and entertainment, sex sells and sexiness equals ratings, because most women secretly have a desire to be attractive like the woman on television, while most men are attracted to a woman who is more visually appealing. But while sexy may be right for the television anchor or actress, it is not the right look for a female corporate executive.

For men, sitting styles include feet close to one another on the floor with knees spread slightly, (Fig. 27.5) feet on the floor with knees spread wider than the feet, (Fig. 27.6) one leg on the floor with the ankle of the other leg placed on the knee, (Fig. 27.7) and sitting with knees crossed in the same way as described above as the women's scissors or inverted V style. (Fig. 27.8)

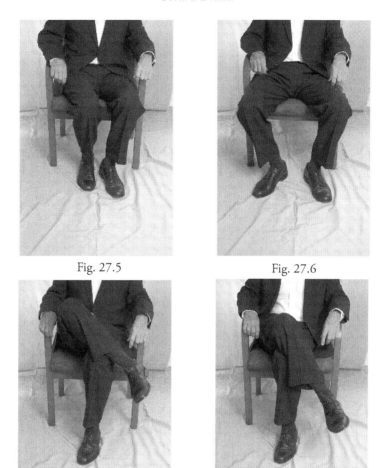

Fig. 27.5   Fig. 27.6

Fig. 27.7   Fig. 27.8

The most offensive of these four male seating types is the legs spread wide open, (Fig. 27.6) essentially making his genitals the focal point of his posture. Many athletes tend to sit like this in interviews. While such posture might be fine in the locker room, it never works in an interview. The male sitting with his legs wide open sends a message of overconfidence and high superiority. And while that may intentionally or subliminally be the message the male is trying to send, a reporter or television audience may also interpret it as a sign of ignorance or stupidity.

A man crossing one ankle over his knee, almost in the shape of a number 4, is the most common posture for men and is often acceptable in interviews, but it is not without its problems. (Fig. 27.7) The exposed sole of your shoe could prove to be an embarrassment, especially if it turns out that a hole has started to develop on the shoe sole below the ball of your foot. Other times, you may have stepped in gum, which leaves a mark on the shoe sole. There are also multi-cultural considerations when a man sits like this. In many Asian and Muslim cultures, exposing the sole of your shoe is a great insult, so think carefully about your audience before sitting like this.

Men older than 40 tend to be more likely to cross their legs at the knee, in the inverted V style, than younger men. (Fig. 27.8) From a body language perspective, many people perceive this seating style to be more feminine, especially in younger men, even to the point of being stereotyped as being homosexual. For younger men, such posture may even be perceived as a sign of weakness. For older men, there is sometimes a degree of maturity or wisdom associated with this type of leg crossing. A key indicator of whether this type of leg crossing has a feminine or masculine appearance depends upon how far out and how high up the raised foot is. The closer the raised foot is to the low leg, the more feminine the appearance. The more raised the foot is in relation to the lower leg, the more masculine the appearance. This more raised approach is really a cross between the number 4 style and the inverted V style. One advantage this has to the pure number 4 style is that it points the shoe sole to the floor, shielding under-shoe blemishes and eliminating cultural insensitivity.

For both men and women, the best posture for sitting is to bring your back slightly away from the back of the chair, which also pushes your posterior slightly forward on the seat of the chair (Fig. 27.9 & Fig. 27.10). With your body weight shifted forward, it virtually forces your feet to the floor, rather than having your legs crossed. Once your feet are comfortably on the floor, men generally slide one foot slightly more forward than the other. Women will do the same in some cases, but in most cases will now find it more comfortable to cross one foot behind the other. When attempting this style, you should not be sitting on the edge of the chair, but just slightly away from the back of the chair.

Fig. 27.9   Fig. 27.10

This slightly forward seating posture also makes it more possible for you to talk with your hands during an interview. Talking with your hands, especially with your palms in an upward position, is a sign of openness and honesty. It lets you gesture with palms up to the interviewer when directing outward expressions, while gesturing with palms up toward yourself for personal stories or to demonstrate personal accountability.

Among the things never to do with your hands in an interview is to flail them or pass them in front of your face. You should also avoid crossing your hands on your lap. Flailing is an indication that you are somewhat sporadic and lack focus. Crossing your hands over your lap and genitals indicates weakness for men and women. For men, having their hands crossed over their genitals is a big sign of feeling vulnerable.

Not only is crossing your hands over your genitals an incorrect posture when you are sitting, it is also incorrect when standing. Commonly referred to as the fig leaf position, hands over the genitals for a male, again, is a sign of weakness and vulnerability, as well as weakness for a woman. Many people instinctively cross their hands over their genitals when standing because this is the way they have taken so many group photos from the time they were in grade school. As an adult, it is time for you to learn that this is an old trick used by photographers to get children to stand still and keep their hands to themselves long enough for the photographer to snap the exposure. The trick kept Billy from punching Bobby on the arm while the children were positioned as a group. And from a photo perspective, crossed hands is never good photography.

Also, while standing, you should avoid swaying back and forth. This demonstrates the same type of nervousness as swaying or swiveling in a chair. The preferred posture when standing is to have your feet spread slightly or to place your weight on your dominant leg.

Many people are also confused about what to do with their hands during an interview when they are standing. In addition to avoiding the fig leaf position, you should never put your hands in your pockets. Placing your hands on your hips comes naturally for some people, but from a body language perspective it is perceived as a sign of arrogance or superiority. Generally the best default position is to have your hands at your side then raise them between your waist and chest for gesturing. When not gesturing, a good standby position is to have your hands lying one inside the other just above the waist, waiting for the next opportunity to talk with your hands and gesture.

To wrap things up, your words will always be important, but whether the reporter or his audience believes you will depend in part on your body language.

In our next lesson, we'll answer that age-old question: should you speak off the record? I'll tell you the answer if you promise not to tell anyone.

.

LESSON 28:
SPEAKING OFF THE RECORD

Never agree to speak off the record.

This lesson really could end with just that phrase: Never speak off the record.

Speaking off the record has been taboo among the wisest media trainers and public relations sages for decades, but rarely do I teach a media training class in which I don't get asked if it is okay to speak off of the record. Furthermore, the question is usually asked by someone who thinks speaking off of the record is a good idea.

Let's go back to 7th grade. Johnny likes Suzie. Johnny confesses to Suzie's best friend, Mary, that he likes Suzie. Johnny admonishes Mary not to tell anyone. Within an hour the entire 7th grade class knows Johnny likes Suzie.

Now that you are an adult, do you think the rules and practices of confidentiality have changed? They have not.

Speaking off of the record is triggered by either an incentive from the spokesperson or a suggestion from the reporter. It usually happens when the interview reaches an impasse because the spokesperson knows that if he says more, his comments will compromise a relationship or expose confidential information. Sometimes the spokesperson would like the information to be known publicly, but not be associated with him.

When the discussion reaches an impasse, the reporter might suggest, "Would you be willing to tell me off the record?" Sometimes the spokesperson might initiate the agreement by suggesting, "If I tell you, can we keep it off the record?"

The inference is that once spoken, the reporter will simply sit on the information as though it helps paint a clearer picture of what is perhaps an incomplete story. Don't believe it. Don't do it.

A reporter will always, in some way, use the information. Perhaps in their report they'll say, "confidential sources tell us," then share the information. Anyone close to the topic can likely do enough deductive reasoning to trace the information back to you, which ultimately damages your reputation. Sometimes the reporter dangles your information in front of another source as an incentive to get the other source to say "on the record" what you would not say "off the record." To me, it all adds up to bad ethics.

Some individuals will share information off the record as a way to get a reporter to attack an opponent or competitor. This often happens in politics and the corporate world. Again, to me it is bad ethics. If you have charges to level, say them for the entire world to hear and be prepared to back up what you say. If you can't back it up, you shouldn't be saying it.

Back in my days in journalism school at Louisiana Tech University, my mentors taught that as a reporter, if someone told you something off of the record, your only choice was to take that information to the grave with you. Using the information to pry information from someone else was unethical. Furthermore, we were taught that as reporters we should not ask anyone to go off the record, because someone else might tell us the same information "on the record." If someone told us the same information on the record after we first went off the record with a prior source, the prior source might very well think we compromised his trust or confidence.

Speaking off the record creates a bevy of problems and sets the stage for a variety of ethical pitfalls, all of which can be avoided by always speaking only for the record.

Akin to speaking off the record is when a reporter will ask you to speak on background. This infers again that your comments will better help the reporter understand all of the facts, and in many ways infers the reporter will not quote you. It subtly implies confidentiality but really means the reporter will in fact use the information to garner more facts from another source.

I don't like the vagueness of "speaking on background" and I would advise you to avoid this practice as well.

If you believe something and you have the proof to back it up, then say it. If you can't prove it or support your position, then hold your tongue.

Let good ethics be your guide.

In our next lesson, I'll tie up everything with some concluding thoughts.

LESSON 29:
CONCLUSION

We began this 29 lesson discussion with the admonition, "Don't talk to the media." The original admonition was that you speak through the media to your audience and the media's audience.

But as we conclude, let me take this thought a bit further. We've poured out for you 29 lessons of best practices for dealing with the media. These practices are tried and true. They work. Please use them.

If you deviate from any of these lessons, you will likely face consequences that damage you, your reputation and the financial health of your organization, whether it be government, non-profit or corporate.

My mentors and personal business coaches always tell me that if I want to achieve higher successes, I should hang around with and learn from people who have achieved the success I would like to achieve. My personal business coaches are the people I turn to in order to learn skills I don't currently have, or to coach me through improving certain skills that need improving. My coaches remind me also that just as great athletes and performers practice constantly, so must all of us practice a variety of skills in order to be better at them.

Dealing with the media and doing interviews with the media is not easy for most people. Some make it look easy, but those are the ones who have great coaches and who have taken the time to practice on many occasions.

I hope the information in these lessons is useful to you. I encourage you to hire a personal media trainer or coach to take your skills to the next level. Don't allow yourself to feel embarrassed because you are asking for help and be willing to exercise a degree of humility if you don't meet your own expectations in the early stages of training. Furthermore, I encourage you to make training and practice a regular part of your professional career. Media training is not something that you put on a list, then check off as completed because you have done it once. Learning the skill of talking to the media requires a commitment to training over many years.

If, on the other hand, you chose not to take the advice that has been so freely shared with you in these lessons, at least take this piece of advice: Don't talk to the media.

KEYNOTES & PRIVATE MEDIA TRAINING

Gerard Braud is passionate about the written and spoken word. If you would like Gerard to deliver a keynote speech to your company or association, please check for pricing and availability at www.BraudCommunications.com

Gerard Braud is available to conduct private and group media training for your executives and employees. For pricing and availability, please visit www.BraudCommunications.com

ADDITIONAL RESOURCES

Don't Talk to the Media is available as a full audio learning system. To purchase your companion audio lessons, please visit www.braudcasting.com

You may wish to make a bulk purchase of both the Don't Talk to the Media book and audio lessons for distribution to the executives where you work.

Please visit these websites for additional resources and training programs:

www.DontTalkToTheMedia.com
www.BraudCommunications.com
www.ExecutiveMediaTraining.com
www.BraudCasting.com
www.CrisisCommunicationsPlans.com
www.SchoolCrisisPlan.com
www.KatrinaLessons.com

Gerard Braud

4971987R0

Made in the USA
Charleston, SC
12 April 2010